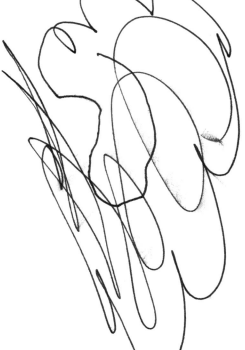

THE OFFICIAL
PRO FOOTBALL HALL of FAME
ANSWER BOOK

Joe Horrigan

SIMON AND SCHUSTER BOOKS FOR YOUNG READERS
Published by Simon & Schuster Inc.
New York

The views expressed in this book are solely
those of the author and do not necessarily
represent those of the Pro Football Hall of Fame.

Photos appear courtesy of NFL Properties, Inc.,
and the Pro Football Hall of Fame, excepting the photo on page 10, which
appears courtesy of Wide World, and the photo on
page 81, which appears courtesy of the Bettmann Archive.

A TOUCHDOWN PUBLICATIONS BOOK

SIMON AND SCHUSTER
BOOKS FOR YOUNG READERS
Simon & Schuster Building
Rockefeller Center
1230 Avenue of the Americas
New York, NY 10020
Copyright © 1990 by Touchdown Publications,
A Division of Robert R. McCord & Associates, Inc.
All rights reserved
including the right of reproduction
in whole or in part in any form.
SIMON AND SCHUSTER BOOKS FOR YOUNG READERS
is a trademark of Simon & Schuster Inc.
Also available in a Little Simon paperback edition
Manufactured in the United States of America
10 9 8 7 6 5 4 3 2 1
ISBN: 0–671–71001–X
          0–671–68695–X (pbk).

Contents

What was the worst team in NFL history?

If you consider only won-lost records, several National Football League teams might be worthy of the title "worst." After all, twenty-one different NFL teams have gone an entire season without a win. Most were teams from the league's early years. Many lasted just one or two seasons before folding. Some winless teams were victims of the severe player shortage caused by World War II military service. More recently, the 1960 Dallas Cowboys and the 1976 Tampa Bay Buccaneers had winless seasons (though Dallas did manage to tie one game). However, both these teams were expansion teams. Few really expected them to win many games—if any at all—in their first seasons.

My choice for the worst NFL team, however, wasn't an expansion team, or one from the league's early years, or one affected by a player shortage. And believe it or not, it wasn't even a winless team. But, boy, were the 1952 Dallas Texans a bad team.

The Texans were a transplanted version of another pretty bad team, the New York Yanks, who had been sold and moved to Dallas after eight losing seasons in New York. Their fresh start in Dallas began on a rather sour note. Only 17,499 fans showed up to see the Texans' regular season debut against the New York Giants. Amazingly, the Texans scored first. But the Giants quickly bounced back and trounced Dallas, 24–6.

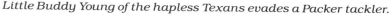

Little Buddy Young of the hapless Texans evades a Packer tackler.

Things went from bad to worse. As the Texans lost game after game, the crowds got smaller and smaller. Finally, after a seventh consecutive loss and with virtually no fans, the team's owners called it quits. NFL Commissioner Bert Bell announced that the league was taking over the Texans' franchise and that the Texans would finish the season as a road team.

After lopsided losses to the Detroit Lions and the Green Bay Packers, the Texans shocked the pro football world by defeating the Chicago Bears, 27–23.

The game was played in Akron, Ohio, as the second part of a Thanksgiving Day doubleheader. Although there was a full house for the first game, between two area high schools, only a few hundred stayed for the pro game. Legend has it that Texans coach Jimmy Phelan suggested that, rather than have his team introduced to the tiny crowd, they should go up to the stands to "meet each fan individually."

Phelan, according to many of his former players, was a truly wonderful man who, even in defeat, kept his sense of humor. Former Texans player Art Donovan once recalled how Phelan reacted to the Dallas Texans' very last touchdown. It occurred in the last game of the 1952 season. Trailing the Detroit Lions, 41–0, with just a few minutes left to play, the Texans managed to score. Phelan, according to Donovan, jumped up and yelled, "Okay, boys, we got 'em on the run now."

Unfortunately, Phelan's sense of humor wasn't enough to save the Dallas Texans. For the season they scored only 182 points, while giving up an amazing 427. They missed seven extra-point attempts and all four of their field goal attempts.

When the 1952 season was mercifully over, the Texans went out of business, the last time an NFL franchise would ever do so. As a final indication of just how bad they were, twenty Texan players never played pro football again. Amazingly, though, a few went on to have outstanding NFL careers, including Art Donovan and Gino Marchetti. Both are now members of the Pro Football Hall of Fame.

How did the Super Bowl get started?

The predecessor of the Super Bowl was the NFL Championship Game, which began in 1933, when the NFL was divided into the Eastern and Western divisions. The winners of each division, the New York Giants in the East and the Chicago Bears in the West, met on December 17 at Wrigley Field in Chicago for the first NFL Championship Game, with the Bears winning, 23–21, on a fourth-quarter Bronko Nagurski TD pass. The NFL Championship Game determined the NFL champ for many years.

When the American Football League began in 1960, it featured its own AFL Championship Game between the winners of the Eastern and Western divisions. The first AFL Championship Game, between the Houston Oilers and the San Diego Chargers, was decided by three TD passes by George Blanda, with the Oilers winning, 24–16.

For the next few years, each league had its own championship game, but the warring leagues refused to compete against each other on the field. This all changed after the 1966 season, when the winners of the NFL Championship Game met the winners at the AFL Championship Game in the first Super Bowl, on January 15, 1967.

Each year after that the champions of the rival leagues met to decide the World Championship. When the AFL and NFL merged in 1970, the NFL divided into two conferences: the AFC and the NFC. Now the Super Bowl is played between the champions of the two conferences.

The first four Super Bowls were played before the two leagues merged. At that time, AFL fans were sure that their league, which had only been around since 1960, was ready to take on the older NFL. NFL fans didn't think so. After the NFL's Green Bay Packers beat the AFL's Kansas City Chiefs, 35–10, in Super Bowl I, most of the public and the press didn't think so either. Those who still favored the AFL were even more disappointed the next year, when the Packers beat the Oakland Raiders, 33–14, in Super Bowl II.

In the days leading up to Super Bowl III things looked even worse for the AFL. Sportswriters were predicting another NFL blowout. Some predicted the NFL champion Baltimore Colts would beat the AFL champion New York Jets by as much as 47 points. However, the cocky Jets' quarterback, Joe Namath, "guaranteed" that his team would win. Namath's brash statement made national headlines and created even more interest in the game. When the Jets beat the Colts, 16–7, not only did the AFL win its first Super Bowl, but it proved to millions of viewers that "the other league" was ready for the NFL.

The following year, the AFL won its second Super Bowl. The Kansas City Chiefs defeated the Minnesota Vikings, 23–7, in Super Bowl IV. For the Chiefs, it was a chance to prove they were better than their Super Bowl I score suggested. And for the entire AFL, it meant respect. This was the last Super Bowl played before the merger. After four Super Bowls, the score was tied: NFL two, AFL two.

Did you know that the first two Super

How the SUPER BOWL was named

"SHARRON, MY SEVEN-YEAR-OLD DAUGHTER, HAD A TOY CALLED A SUPER BALL . . . IN THE AFL-NFL JOINT COMMITTEE MEETINGS, WE HAD BEEN REFERRING TO THE 'FINAL GAME.' SUBCONSCIOUSLY, I MAY HAVE BEEN THINKING ABOUT SHARRON'S TOY AND ONE DAY I JUST HAPPENED TO COME OUT AND CALL THE GAME THE 'SUPER BOWL.' SOMEHOW OR OTHER, THE NAME JUST STUCK."

LAMAR HUNT, PRESIDENT
KANSAS CITY CHIEFS

SUPER BALL

COMMISSIONER PETE ROZELLE AND LAMAR HUNT AT THE SUPER BOWL.

This photo of an exhibit at the Hall tells the whole story.

Bowls weren't called Super Bowls? That's right. Originally, the game was called the AFL-NFL World Championship Game. A committee of owners from both leagues decided that a special name for the game was needed and several names were considered. It was Lamar Hunt, owner of the Kansas City Chiefs, who came up with the term "Super Bowl" after remembering a toy ball his daughter would play with called a "super ball."

What's the difference
between a Pro Bowl team and an All-Pro team?

As I'm sure you know, being selected for a Pro Bowl team or to an All-Pro team is a great honor for a player. Both are a means of recognizing players as the best at their positions during a season. Often a player is selected for both teams. So what's the difference? Well, it's a matter of who selects them and how.

The AFC-NFC Pro Bowl teams are selected by ballot of the head coaches and players in each conference. Each team has two equal votes. One vote is that of the head coach, while the other is a consensus of the players' votes. The coaches and players vote only for players in their conference and may not vote for players on their own team. Each Pro Bowl team has a forty-one man roster that is selected in this manner. A forty-second player, called a "need player," is named to each squad by the Pro Bowl head coaches. The "need player" is a cornerback or a safety unless the coach can clearly establish that a greater need exists at another position, such as punt returner or kickoff returner. These players who are selected play in the annual AFC-NFC Pro Bowl Game, which is usually held in Hawaii two weeks after the Super Bowl.

Unlike the Pro Bowl teams, All-Pro teams are not considered *official* NFL teams. All-Pro teams are not selected by players or coaches and there is no All-Pro Game. In fact, there are several All-Pro teams selected each year. The three that are recognized by the NFL are chosen by the Pro Football Writers of America, the Associated Press, and the United Press International.

The UPI names two separate teams: the All-AFC team and the All-NFC team. Both the AP and PFWA name combined AFC-NFC All-Pro teams.

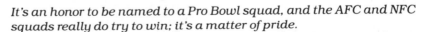

It's an honor to be named to a Pro Bowl squad, and the AFC and NFC squads really do try to win; it's a matter of pride.

8

Being named to a Pro Bowl squad means that your peers think you're one of the best.

What is artificial turf?

Artificial turf is a generic term used to describe the several different types of synthetic playing surfaces. The best way to describe it is that it's like a huge carpet made of grasslike fibers. This carpet is applied over a cushion or shock-absorbing pad, which is usually applied over an asphalt base. The purpose of artificial turf is to replace real grass, which can quickly turn to mud when a game is played in inclement weather. Artificial turf also allows stadium owners to schedule other events in the stadium without having to resod the entire field each time.

The first artificial turf appeared on the sports scene in 1966, when the builders of the Houston Astrodome discovered that grass won't grow in a domed stadium. Baseball's Houston Astros, the Astrodome's tenants, actu-ally considered playing on an all-dirt field. Then Astros owner Judge Roy Hofheinz read a brief article describing an experimental synthetic playing surface known as ChemGrass. Hofheinz and the ChemGrass manufacturer, the Monsanto Company, made a deal. Monsanto agreed to install the experimental playing surface free of charge and Hofheinz agreed to allow Monsanto to market the product worldwide as AstroTurf.

In 1968, when the Houston Oilers made the Astrodome their home field, they became the first pro football team to have a home field with an artificial playing surface. Since then, several other NFL stadiums have installed AstroTurf, or a similar type of artificial playing surface.

God's green grass won't grow under glass, so the man-made stuff prevails.

How does the football draft work?

Although there have been some changes over the years, the draft still works in much the same way it did in 1936, when it was first introduced after being suggested by Philadelphia Eagles owner Bert Bell, who later became the commissioner of the National Football League. He designed the draft to help balance the power in the league and saw it as a way for the weaker teams to get stronger. Here's how it works.

Every year the best players coming out of the college ranks are selected, or "drafted," by NFL teams. Each team selects one player until all twenty-eight teams have made a choice. This is repeated twelve times, or through twelve "rounds." The team that picks first in each round is the team that finished the previous season with the worst record. The second pick is made by the team with the second worst, and so on, until all twenty-eight teams have made a pick. The Super Bowl champion always picks last.

In the early years of the draft, there was very little preparation. In fact, a draft meeting was more like an informal get-together of the NFL owners. At the first draft meeting in 1936, a list of approximately ninety players, largely

It's a thrill for a collegiate star (like Tom Nowatzke of Indiana) to be selected by the pros.

taken from newspaper and magazine articles and All-America lists, was scribbled on a blackboard. Teams had to draft from this list. By comparison, teams today have full-time scouting staffs that keep records on more than nine thousand potential draft choices. There are also draft combines that provide information to all teams subscribing to the service.

Some strange twists have taken place on draft day in the NFL. For instance, in 1956, the Cleveland Browns intended to draft a quarterback in the first round to replace the recently retired Otto Graham. The Los Angeles Rams had the first pick, followed by the San Francisco 49ers. The Browns, Green Bay Packers, and Pittsburgh Steelers were all tied in the standings for the third pick. Two coin tosses were used to break the tie. Cleveland lost both and had to settle for the fifth spot in the first round. As a result, the Browns had to sit by and watch as the two best college quarterbacks available that year—Stanford's John Brodie and Purdue's Len Dawson—were drafted. When it came time for the Browns to make their selection, since both the quarterbacks they wanted had already been selected, they decided to settle for Syracuse fullback Jim Brown. *Settle for Brown?* Talk about a steal! Jim Brown not only led the league in rushing in his rookie season, but when he retired in 1965 he was the NFL's all-time leading rusher.

When did pro football play its first game indoors?

It might surprise you to discover that the first indoor pro football game was played in what was called the "world series." If you thought only baseball teams played in the World Series, you're mistaken. In 1902, the manager of Madison Square Garden, a clever New York promoter named Tom O'Rourke, was looking for a way to fill his arena on New Year's Day, 1903. He came up with the idea of playing a series of indoor football games, the winner of which, he declared, would be the World Champion.

The best pro teams in 1902 had been the Phillies and Athletics of Philadelphia, the Stars of Pittsburgh, and the Red and Blacks of Watertown, New York. Unfortunately, O'Rourke was unable to get any of those teams to play in his indoor series. The Phillies, Athletics, and Red and Blacks turned down invitations, while the Stars weren't even invited.

However, players from both the Phillies and Athletics got together and formed a new team, which they named the "New York" team. The other teams scheduled to play were the Orange, New Jersey, Athletic Club; the Warlow Athletic Club; the New York Knickerbockers; and the Syracuse Athletic Club.

O'Rourke's plan was to set up a schedule that would allow the favored hometown Knickerbockers to play the neighboring Orange Athletic Club in the final Championship Game. This, he thought, would guarantee a better turnout of fans on New Year's Day. So, wanting to eliminate the weaker teams early, O'Rourke scheduled the Syracuse Athletic Club and the "New York" team to open the series and play

Alas, no picture of the historic 1902 indoor football contest in Madison Square Garden has survived. Above is a panoramic view of today's Astrodome.

pro football's first indoor game on December 28, 1902.

O'Rourke assumed ''New York'' would defeat Syracuse and then the stronger Knickerbockers would defeat both the weak Warlow Athletic Club and then the ''New York'' team. However, what O'Rourke didn't count on was Syracuse loading up its roster with stars from other teams, including the entire backfield of the powerful Watertown Red and Blacks.

The bolstered Syracuse Athletic Club not only won its opener, 5–0, but clobbered both the Knickerbockers and Orange Athletic Club by 36–0 scores and claimed the 1902 indoor World Championship.

What was the "Heidi game"?

On November 17, 1968, at 7 P.M., NBC began its telecast of the popular family movie *Heidi*, a story about a young Swiss girl, right on schedule. The problem was that in order to do so, NBC had had to leave a crucial football game between the Oakland Raiders and New York Jets while there was still 1:03 left to play.

The NBC switchboard instantly lit up with calls from angry fans all over the country. Not only had NBC cut off the game, but they cut it off before the final score was decided. When NBC left the game, the Jets were ahead, 32–29. However, in the last forty-two seconds, while Heidi was picking edelweiss and milking goats in the Alps, the Raiders scored two touchdowns to win, 43–32.

NBC could do little more than apologize and promise that it wouldn't happen again. They meant it: Less than a month later, the network delayed by eight minutes the movie *Huckleberry Finn* so football fans would see the San Diego Chargers–Oakland Raiders game in its entirety.

Who were the smallest and largest players to play in the NFL?

It is often said that pro football is a big man's sport. There's no denying that some big men have played the game, but the little man has also made his mark.

In 1974, the New England Patriots' five-foot-five running back Mack Herron gained a record 2,444 combined net yards. Twelve years later, the San Diego Chargers' five-foot-six all-purpose back Lionel James bettered that mark by 91 yards.

However, Herron and James weren't the smallest players ever to play in the National Football League. That distinction goes to Jack Shapiro. Jack, who played halfback for the NFL's 1929 Staten Island Stapletons, was a mere five feet and one-half inch tall.

In a letter he wrote to the Hall of Fame in 1980, Shapiro explained that most rosters listed his height incorrectly at five-feet-five. As proof of his claim, he sent the Hall a copy of his Army discharge paper that does indeed list him as five feet and one-half inch. He also wrote that, to the best of his recollection, he weighed 121 pounds when he played pro ball.

The largest man to play in the NFL is

Was Les Bingaman the NFL's biggest man?

13

more difficult to determine. At seven feet, former Oakland Raiders defensive tackle Richard Sligh was probably the tallest. But, weighing "just" 300 pounds, he certainly wasn't the heaviest.

Once a rarity in pro football, the 300-pound player is quickly becoming common. Perhaps the best-known 300-pounder of recent years is Chicago Bears defensive tackle William (the Refrigerator) Perry. The Fridge, who has had to work hard to control his weight, has drifted above the 325-pound mark on several occasions. Just how much beyond that mark is uncertain.

In the 1960s, New York Jets coach, Weeb Ewbank would try to motivate 325-pound tackle Sherman Plunkett to get down to 300 by offering him a $2,000 bonus. It never worked. "Getting around Plunkett," a rival coach once remarked, "is like taking a trip around the world."

Perhaps the NFL's heaviest player, though, was Les Bingaman, a middle guard with the Detroit Lions from 1948 to 1954. Some say he weighed as much as 350 pounds. However, no one seems to know for sure. Bucko Kilroy, who played against him, claims the Lions had to take him to the general store to weigh him. Maybe they had to feed him there too.

What was pro football's most unusual team?

In the history of the game, there never was a team quite like the Oorang Indians. Members of the National Football League in 1922–23, the Oorang Indians were organized by Walter Lingo, the owner of the Oorang Kennels in the small town of LaRue, Ohio. Lingo organized the team for the sole purpose of advertising his kennel and selling a breed of dog known as the Airedale.

Besides his dogs, Lingo had another great interest—the American Indian. So the kennel owner hired the fabled American Indian Jim Thorpe to line up and coach an entire squad of Indian athletes. Indians came from all over the country to try out for Lingo's team. Many came from Thorpe's old school, Carlisle. When the roster was complete, it included such names as Big Bear, Joe Little Twig, Long-Time-Sleep, and War Eagle.

Since Lingo's plan was to advertise his dogs and kennel, the Indians rarely played at home. In fact, tiny LaRue had no football field, so when they did play a "home game," it was played in neighboring Marion, Ohio.

The Indians were not a very good team. In fact, they won only three games during their two years in the NFL. I'm sure the players found it difficult to take their football seriously when you consider what Lingo had in mind. The pregame and halftime activities were more important to him than the results of the games.

Entertainment, both prior to the games and during halftimes, was provided by the players and the Airedale dogs. There were shooting exhibitions with the dogs retrieving the targets. There were Indian dances and tomahawk and knife-throwing demonstrations. It's said that one player, Nikolas Lassa, called Long-Time-Sleep by his teammates, even wrestled a bear on occasion.

At first, the Oorang Indians were an excellent gate attraction. However, af-

The Oorang Indians featured such stars as Jim Thorpe (back row, center). Pete Calac (back row, right), and Joe Guyon (front row, third from left).

ter two years, the novelty of an all-Indian team began to wear out. With crowds getting smaller each week, Lingo decided to pull out. So, at the end of the 1923 season, the Oorang Indians, undoubtedly pro football's most unusual team, folded their tents and closed down the show for good.

Have there been any other pro leagues besides the NFL?

Yes, indeed. Seven different leagues have challenged the National Football League since its inception in 1920.

The first three challengers, though not related, were all known as the American Football League. The first AFL was started in 1926 by ex-Chicago Bears running back Red Grange and his manager, C. C. (Cash-and-Carry) Pyle, after the two failed to gain part ownership of the Bears and the NFL refused them a franchise in New York City. They believed that Grange, the biggest name in football at the time, would fill stadiums in any league. Al-though Grange's team, the New York Yankees, did well, the rest of the league was a disaster. Five of the league's nine teams folded before the season ended. The rest packed it in after just one season.

The second AFL lasted only two years (1936–37) and never had more than six teams. The league's first Championship Game between the Boston Shamrocks and Cleveland Rams was canceled when the Boston players refused to play because they were owed pay for past games.

Of all the leagues to challenge the

NFL, the 1940–41 AFL was probably the weakest. By the time it folded, membership in the league was down to five teams. One, the Cincinnati Bengals (no relation to the present-day Bengals), actually forfeited a game when they were unable to come up with enough players.

The next league to challenge the NFL was the All-America Football Conference of 1946–49. The AAFC was much more successful than any of the first three AFLs. This league produced the Cleveland Browns, the San Francisco 49ers, the original Baltimore Colts, and a host of players—including several future Hall of Famers—who went on to star in the NFL.

For four years, the AAFC and the NFL waged a costly war. Finally, after the 1949 season, the AAFC agreed to the NFL's terms for a merger. The Browns, 49ers, and Colts were taken into the NFL. Through a complicated system, the players from the remaining AAFC teams were divided up among the established NFL teams. The "merger" was in truth more like a surrender by the AAFC.

In 1960, the fourth American Football League was born. This new league proved to be the NFL's most serious competitor. Led by wealthy young businessmen, this AFL immediately challenged the older NFL in signing player talent. With a wide-open style of play, it was an exciting league to watch. Several outstanding players, including Hall of Famers Lance Alworth and Joe Namath, got their start in the AFL. The young league also found success in several cities that had been shunned by the older NFL. Because of the AFL, in just one decade, pro football grew from twelve teams to twenty-six. Cities such as Buffalo, New York, and Miami, Florida, which hadn't had pro football teams since the AAFC

It was smiles all around for the Cleveland Browns after they won the 1946 AAFC championship, their first of four straight.

The Dolphins were not Miami's only entry in a rival league; here are the Miami Seahawks of the 1946 AAFC.

years, were once again members of the pro football family.

In 1966, a merger between the AFL and NFL was agreed upon. Beginning in 1970, the AFL would be known as the American Football Conference and the NFL would become the National Football Conference. Together the two conferences would make up the NFL.

Also, as part of the merger agreement, beginning with the 1966 season, an annual Championship Game between the AFL and the NFL would be played. This annual Championship Game is now known as the Super Bowl and is played between the AFC and NFC champions.

The NFL's next rival league, the World Football League, lasted only one full season (1974) and a part of a sec-

ond (1975) before folding. For the most part, this league was an embarrassment. One team, the Detroit Wheels, actually had to borrow athletic tape from another team and the players had to bring their own towels to games.

The most recent pro football league was known as the United States Football League, or the USFL. Originally, the USFL was a spring league. However, after three mildly successful spring seasons, it decided to challenge the NFL and play in the fall. The strategy didn't work. Unable to get a necessary television contract, the league folded. However, the USFL did produce its share of stars, such as Herschel Walker, Jim Kelly, and Reggie White. Several are still active with NFL teams.

What was the longest game ever played in NFL history?

The record for the longest game goes to the 1971 AFC divisional playoff game between the Kansas City Chiefs and the Miami Dolphins. Played on Christmas Day, the seesaw battle of touchdowns and field goals didn't end until halfway through the sixth quarter. The double-overtime game lasted eighty-two minutes and forty seconds. It was one of the most exciting games ever played. Here's how it happened.

The Chiefs scored the first two times they had the ball and led, 10–0, at the end of the first quarter. In the second quarter, the Dolphins added 10 points of their own. At halftime, the score was tied, 10–10.

Both teams scored touchdowns in the third quarter. In the fourth, the Chiefs scored another to take the lead, 24–17. However, with 1:25 remaining in regulation play, the Dolphins again tied the game up. On the next play, Chiefs running back Ed Podolak returned the Dolphins' kickoff 78 yards to the Miami 22-yard line. Three more plays advanced the ball to the 15. Now, with just thirty-five seconds left and sensing a victory, Jan Stenerud attempted a game-winning field goal. The kick was up and . . . no good! With the score tied, 24–24, the remaining seconds ticked away. With Christmas dinners getting cold and millions of moms' patience wearing thin, the game went into overtime.

In the fifth quarter, both teams missed scoring opportunities. Stenerud had a 42-yard field goal attempt blocked and Dolphins placekicker Garo Yepremian missed a 52-yarder. Finally, halfway through the sixth quarter, Yepremian got another chance. This

Runner Ed Podolak tore up the field, but his Kansas City Chiefs came up short of the win.

time his 37-yard attempt was good and the Dolphins won, 27–24.

Though his team didn't win, the real star that day was Chiefs running back Ed Podolak. In one of the greatest post-season performances in the history of pro football, Podolak carried the ball 17 times for 85 yards, caught 8 passes for 110 yards, returned 3 kickoffs for 153 yards, and ran back 2 punts for 2 yards. For the day, Podolak gained a combined total of 350 yards.

Has an NFL team ever had an undefeated season?

In 1920, the Akron Pros, the NFL's first champions, posted an undefeated 8–0–3 record. The Canton Bulldogs, with their undefeated season records of 10–0–2 in 1922 and 11–0–1 in 1923, were the first NFL team to win consecutive league titles. And in 1929, the Green Bay Packers won the first of their three consecutive NFL titles with an undefeated record of 12–0–1. However, each of these teams played at least one tie game.

It's not a coincidence that these undefeated teams were league champions. Up until 1933, the NFL title was decided by a team's won-lost record. There was no Championship Game or Super Bowl the way there is today.

With a 13–0 record, the 1934 Chicago Bears were the first NFL team to go undefeated and untied in the regular season. They featured an explosive offense led by rookie running back Beattie Feathers. Feathers was the first running back in NFL history to rush for more than 1,000 yards in a season. His 1,004 yards on just 101 carries is one of the game's most remarkable records and his 9.94 average gain per carry is still an NFL record. Imagine: Feathers averaged nearly enough for a first down every time he handled the ball.

In the 1934 NFL Championship Game, the undefeated Bears met the 8–5 New York Giants. To most fans, the game looked like a mismatch. The Bears had already beaten the Giants twice that season. However, an overnight rain, followed by bitter cold in the morning, turned the Polo Grounds field into a sheet of ice.

After an early morning inspection of the field, Giants coach Steve Owen instructed his players to bring their sneakers to the game. Since some players didn't have any, and the sporting goods stores weren't open, a clubhouse equipment man was sent to nearby Manhattan College to borrow additional pairs.

Talk about a smart coach!

The Giants played the entire first half in their regular cleated shoes and both teams were having a terrible time with their footing. Down 10–3 at halftime, Owen decided to make the switch.

A third-quarter field goal extended the Bears' lead to 13–3. However, in the fourth quarter, with the added traction the sneakers provided, the Giants scored four touchdowns and ended the Bears' undefeated record with a 30–13 win. So the Bears, the first NFL team to go undefeated and untied in a regular season, were unable to win the NFL Championship Game and make it a perfect season.

The next NFL team to go undefeated during the regular season was another Chicago Bears team. The Monsters of the Midway, as they were known in 1942, posted an 11–0 record. However,

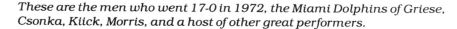

These are the men who went 17-0 in 1972, the Miami Dolphins of Griese, Csonka, Kiick, Morris, and a host of other great performers.

this time the Washington Redskins ruined the Bears' perfect season by defeating them, 14–6, in the Championship Game.

Prior to the game, the Bears were favored by as much as 22 points. Part of the reason might have been that two years earlier, in the 1940 NFL Championship Game, they clobbered the Redskins, 73–0, still the most lopsided score in NFL history. But this time, the Redskins were out for revenge.

One of the truly great teams of the modern era was the 1972 Miami Dolphins football team. Even after losing starting quarterback Bob Griese in the fifth game of the season with a broken ankle, the Dolphins somehow continued to win game after game. While thirty-eight-year-old Earl Morrall filled in nicely for Griese, running backs Mercury Morris and Hall of Famer Larry Csonka rushed for more than 1,000 yards each. Together, they passed, slashed, and pounded their way to a perfect 14–0 regular season.

However, in the AFC Championship Game against the Pittsburgh Steelers, Miami coach Don Shula replaced Morrall with Griese. Though Griese's ankle had healed, he hadn't played in nine weeks. Shula's decision to make the change was a gamble, but the gamble paid off as Griese sparked the Dolphins to a 21–17 win.

Now the big question was: Would Shula start Morrall or Griese in Super Bowl VII? Morrall "was the one who got them there." But the fact was, Griese was the Dolphins' original starting quarterback and Don Shula, who had total confidence in him, selected him to start.

In the first half, leading 14–0, it seemed as though the Dolphins would walk away with an easy win. But late in the fourth quarter, one of the funniest plays in Super Bowl history occurred. Holding on to their slim hope for victory, the Redskins blocked a forty-two-yard Garo Yepremian field goal attempt. Suddenly, the diminutive Yepremian was playing *quarterback*. He scooped up the loose ball and, running for his life, attempted to pass. Unfortunately, the ball wobbled end over end, as if it had a mind of its own, into the outstretched arms of Redskins defensive back Mike Bass, who ran 49 yards for a touchdown. Suddenly, the Redskins were only down by a TD.

However, with just 2:07 remaining in the game, the Dolphins were able to run six plays before having to punt. Starting on their own 30-yard line with 1:14 remaining, the Redskins were unable to get a first down and then the Dolphins simply let the clock run out.

With their 14–7 Super Bowl VII win, the Dolphins became the first and only NFL team to complete the regular and postseason undefeated and untied—a perfect 17–0 season.

When was the first NFL game televised?

The happy marriage between pro football and television began on October 22, 1939. That's when the National Broadcasting Company earned a spot in pro football and television history by becoming the first network to televise a pro football game.

The site was Ebbets Field in Brooklyn, New York, where 13,050 fans witnessed the NFL's Brooklyn

Dodgers defeat the Philadelphia Eagles, 23–14. The game included three future Hall of Famers—quarterback Clarence (Ace) Parker and tackle Frank (Bruiser) Kinard of Brooklyn, and end Bill Hewitt of the Eagles. A reporter for the *New York Times* wrote that Parker and Eagles quarterback Davey O'Brien thrilled the fans with "bulletlike heaves," but no mention was made of the game being televised. As a matter of fact, most of the players didn't even know.

Since there were only about five hundred TV sets in New York at the time, few viewers actually saw the broadcast in their homes. The game was scheduled as a special event for the RCA Pavilion at the World's Fair in New York and many people watched the monitors while the game was in progress.

According to Allen (Skip) Walz, the NBC play-by-play announcer, only eight people were needed for the telecast. It was broadcast over NBC's experimental station, W2XBS. By comparison, it takes a crew of approximately two hundred people to televise the Super Bowl.

Walz had none of the visual aids—monitors, screens, or spotters—used today, and there were just two TV cameras. One was located in the box seats of the 40-yard line and the other was in the stadium balcony.

The television log records for that day say that the game began at 2:30 P.M. and ran for exactly two hours, thirty-three minutes, and ten seconds. By comparison, today's games run almost three full hours. Of course, there were no commercials during the 1939 game.

If the role of television in pro football's history interests you, a good book to read would be *Razzle-Dazzle: The Curious Marriage of Television and Football* by Phil Patton.

Who was the first professional football player?

For many years, it was believed that a young quarterback named John Brallier was the first pro. Brallier, who played for the Latrobe, Pennsylvania, YMCA team, admitted accepting $10 plus expenses for playing in a game on September 3, 1895, against the neighboring Jeanette, Pennsylvania, team. Because no one had ever before publicly admitted to accepting money to play, it was generally assumed that Brallier was the first pro.

However, in 1960, a man named Nelson Ross visited the offices of Pittsburgh Steelers executive Dan Rooney and presented him with a forty-nine-page research paper. Ross told Rooney that he had been researching the roots of pro football for many years and that he had made some discoveries that might interest the NFL. Included was the discovery that William (Pudge) Heffelfinger—not Brallier—was the first pro.

The Ross paper detailed many events that led up to a football game played on November 12, 1892, between two amateur Pittsburgh teams: the Allegheny Athletic Association and the Pittsburgh Athletic Club. According to Ross, this was the game in which Heffelfinger became the first pro.

Apparently, the Pittsburgh Athletic Club (P.A.C.) challenged the Allegheny Athletic Association (A.A.A.) to a game

It all began with Pudge Heffelfinger . . .

posedly to protect his amateur standing, refused the offer. So it was no surprise that a near-riot broke out at the rematch when Heffelfinger appeared on the field for warmups, not as a member of the Pittsburgh Athletic Club but as a member of the Allegheny Athletic Club.

The P.A.C. management insisted that Heffelfinger was being paid by the A.A.A. Of course, the A.A.A. manager O. D. Thompson denied any wrongdoing. After arguing for more than an hour, the two teams agreed to play the game as an exhibition and that "all bets were canceled."

Finally, after all charges and countercharges stopped, the game got under way. And just as the A.A.A.

. . . as proven by this ledger-book page.

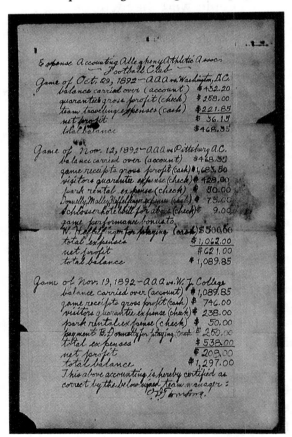

in 1891. The A.A.A. ignored the challenge. This annoyed the P.A.C. Finally, the crosstown rivals agreed to meet on Columbus Day, October 12, 1892. Both sides confidently predicted victory.

More than three thousand excited fans—a large crowd for the day—witnessed the two teams battle to a 6–6 tie. Motivated by the game's success, a rematch was scheduled for November 12.

As the big day for the rematch approached, rumors began to surface that the P.A.C. manager, George Barbour, had offered to pay Heffelfinger, a former three-time All-American guard at Yale who was playing for the Chicago A.A., $250 to play. Heffelfinger, sup-

thought he would be, Heffelfinger was terrific. After recovering a teammate's fumble, he ran 25 yards around end and scored the game's only touchdown. Since touchdowns back then were only worth four points, the A.A.A. won, 4–0.

Heffelfinger never admitted that he was paid to play that day. However, Nelson Ross was convinced that Heffelfinger was a pro. And for good reason . . . he had proof.

Along with the research paper he gave Dan Rooney, Ross included a well-preserved document. It was a page from the accounting ledger of the A.A.A. The official-looking sheet, now on display at the Pro Football Hall of Fame, lists the expenses for three A.A.A. games played in 1892. Included is an entry from the November 12 game that states: "game performance bonus to W. Heffelfinger—for playing (cash) $500." In addition, Heffelfinger and two other players received $25 each for "expenses."

So not only did the Ross research provide valuable information concerning the roots of pro football but also the proof that was needed to document the game's first pro, William (Pudge) Heffelfinger.

Did anyone ever run the wrong way and score for the other team?

Jim Marshall had an outstanding twenty-year NFL career. Yet many people remember him only as "the guy who ran the wrong way."

It happened on October 6, 1964, in a game at San Francisco's Kezar Stadium. In the fourth quarter Marshall, a defensive end for the Minnesota Vikings, recovered a San Francisco 49ers fumble. Recovering fumbles was something of a specialty of Jim's. In fact, he still holds the NFL record (29) for the most opponents' fumbles recovered in a career. This time Marshall scooped up the loose ball and rumbled 66 yards for a score. Unfortunately, he didn't score a touchdown for the Vikings; he scored a safety for the 49ers. Jim Marshall ran 66 yards the wrong way.

As Jim began his wrong-way dash, his teammates were stunned with disbelief. From the sidelines his coaches and teammates screamed and waved their arms wildly. But poor Jim, think-

Impartial Jim Marshall, who helped both sides.

23

ing they were cheering him on, ran even harder. As he got to his own 5-yard line, he saw teammate Fran Tarkenton on the sidelines frantically pointing in the opposite direction. Suddenly, Jim realized what he had done. Confused and unable to think of anything else to do, he threw the ball toward Tarkenton. The useless pass dropped to the ground and rolled out of the end zone for a safety. Adding insult to injury, 49ers center Bruce Bosley immediately shook Marshall's hand and thanked him for the 2-point gift. Despite Marshall's "gift," the Vikings went on to win, 27–22.

A similar play occurred on October 18, 1971, in a game between the Kansas City Chiefs and the Pittsburgh Steelers. This time Steelers wide receiver Dave Smith was the victim. Smith, after catching a pass from quarterback Terry Bradshaw, thought he had crossed the Chiefs' goal line for a touchdown. In celebration, he spiked the ball. However, Smith wasn't in the end zone as he thought but was on the Chiefs' 5-yard line. The spiked fumble bounced through the end zone for a touchback. The Chiefs finished off the Steelers, 38–16.

Adding to Smith's nightmare was the fact that his blunder was viewed by a national TV audience on "Monday Night Football."

Why is a football called a "pigskin"?

Good question. Unfortunately, no one really knows exactly how the term "pigskin" got started. There are two popular theories. First, though, rest assured that footballs are not made from a pig's skin. The preferred material for quality footballs is steerhide. Cowhide is considered second best.

Now for the theories. The first is actually a legend for which there is no historical evidence. A few years after the Danes left England, which they had occupied from about 1016 to 1042, a farmer working in a field uncovered a skull. Guessing that it was the skull of an enemy Dane, he began to kick it around. Soon other workers joined the English farmer kicking the skull up and down the field. Some of the young men found "skull kicking" was a fun way to pass the time. The only problem was that since they wore sandals or shoes of soft leather, "skull kicking"

hurt their toes. A solution was found when somebody replaced the skull with an animal bladder stuffed with straw. Nobody really knows if it was a pig's bladder that was used or if there is any truth to the legend. But the "skull-kicking" theory is at least an entertaining story.

To understand the second theory, you should know that American football is actually a combination of two older sports: soccer and one of its offshoots, rugby. In 1823, during a soccer match at the Rugby School in England, a player named William Webb Ellis, frustrated by his team's inability to kick a goal, picked the ball up and ran over the goal line. This was the first time a player ever ran with the ball. (It wasn't until much later, in 1906, that forward passing was allowed.) This new style of play quickly became popular and was named after the school where it was first played. Of course, a few new rules were added, including one concerning the ball. According to Dr. L. H. Baker, in his book *Football: Facts and Figures*, this is when the term "pigskin" began. He wrote that, in order to make ball-carrying easier, it was decided the rugby ball should be oval instead of round and should be "a leather one, encasing a blown-up bladder." Dr. Baker's theory was that the leather was like a tough pig's skin protecting the soft bladder.

But who knows, maybe instead of being called "a pigskin," a football should be called a "Dane's head."

When did the NFL start?

Even though some players began playing football for money in 1892, the National Football League wasn't established until 1920. There were a lot of reasons why a pro football league was needed, but there were three major ones.

First, there was the problem of salaries. In 1920 salaries were about $50 to $75 a game, and star players were sometimes paid $100 or more. Though not much by today's standards, back then it was enough to bankrupt some teams. In pro football's early years, teams played in small stadiums that were located in small cities and towns. Sometimes a sellout crowd was barely enough to pay the team's salaries and expenses.

Then there was the problem of the players who were jumping from team to team. Some teams would steal another team's star player by paying him more money. Some players even played for more than one team in the same week. It was hard for fans to support their local team when they didn't know if it would have the same players from week to week. Also, by bidding on players, teams drove salaries higher.

The third major problem was that some teams would hire players who were still in college. These players would play college football on Saturday and pro football on Sunday. Because amateur rules prohibited this, they would use fake names when playing pro ball. It was an easy way for a college player to pick up a quick $50 to $100. This caused colleges and the public to distrust the pro game. If pro football wanted to earn the respect of the public, it had to come up with a set of rules. A league seemed like the logical solution.

So on August 20, 1920, in Canton, Ohio, an organizational meeting was held. With just four teams represented, very little was accomplished. However, a second meeting, held on September 17, also in Canton, was much more successful, with representatives from ten teams in attendance. Officers were selected, committees were appointed, and rules to govern the new organization were enacted. It was at this meeting that the American Professional Football Association was born. Two years later, the APFA changed its name to the National Football League.

It was at these early organizational meetings that the NFL's founding fathers established the rules and standards that were necessary to gain and keep the public's trust. Many of these early rules are still in effect today.

Who was Jim Thorpe?

It seems that whenever stories are written about all-time pro football greats, Jim Thorpe's name comes up. Jim Thorpe was born in a one-room cabin in Prague, Oklahoma, on May 28, 1888. Though he had some Irish and French blood, he was of mostly Sac and Fox Indian heritage. In fact, his Indian name was Wa-Tho-Huk, which means Bright Path.

Jim was an all-around athlete. At the Carlisle Indian Industrial School, he excelled at every sport he tried. In 1912, he led his school to a national collegiate football championship.

Though football was his first love, he gained his greatest fame as a track star, winning the decathlon and pentathlon events in the 1912 Olympics, held in Stockholm, Sweden. King Gustav V of Sweden told Thorpe as he presented him with his medals, "Sir, you are the greatest athlete in the world." But soon afterward, Thorpe was stripped of his records and medals when it was learned that he had played minor league baseball for money in 1911. Recently, in 1984, the Olympic Committee decided that this was an unfair interpretation of the then-Olympic rules, and restored his records and returned his medals to his family.

In 1915, Thorpe's great abilities and fame led Jack Cusack to offer him $250 a game to play football for the Canton Bulldogs. While that may not sound like much, it was twice as much as most players were making back then. Even Cusack's friends warned him that he was paying Thorpe too much. Just the same, Thorpe was everything Cusack had hoped he would be—a great player and a great gate attraction. After missing the first two games of the 1916 season because he was playing pro baseball for the New York Giants,

Thorpe joined the Canton squad. With Jim playing halfback, the Bulldogs were unofficial World Champions in 1916, 1917, and 1919. (The Bulldogs' championships are said to be unofficial since

Jim Thorpe, the greatest football player of his day, and perhaps America's greatest athlete ever.

no organized pro league existed at the time.)

Many old-timers who actually played against Thorpe claim he was the toughest man ever to play the game. Some folks claim Jim would dropkick a field goal from the 50-yard line, then turn and kick another 50-yarder in the opposite direction with perfect results—just to show off. Others say he could punt a ball the length of the field. Both are probably exaggerations. In any case, there is no doubt that Thorpe was a superb athlete. All accounts suggest he could run with speed and bruising power. He could pass and catch passes with the best. He could kick with accuracy and strength. And, of course, as players did back then, he played defense too.

By the time the NFL was organized in 1920, the thirty-two-year-old Thorpe, who was already past his athletic prime, was unanimously voted the league's

Thorpe was a one-man gang at the 1912 Olympics, winning the two all-around events.

charter president. However, he managed to play for eight NFL seasons with six different teams and his gate appeal continued. Though at times he sparkled like the Thorpe of old, he never

He also played major-league baseball for six years, batting as high as .327.

really excelled as much in the NFL as he had in his earlier career. In 1928, at the age of forty, he finally called it quits. In 1950, Thorpe was honored by the nation's press by being named the most outstanding athlete of the first fifty years of the twentieth century. In 1963, he was elected a charter member of the Pro Football Hall of Fame.

If you would like to know more about Thorpe, a good book to read is *Jim Thorpe* by Bob Wheeler.

How are players elected to the Pro Football Hall of Fame?

Individuals who are elected to the Pro Football Hall of Fame are the best the game has ever produced. But how they get elected is another story. Charged with that important task is the Hall of Fame's thirty-man Board of Selectors.

The Board of Selectors consist of one media representative from each pro football city. Since New York and Los Angeles each have two teams in the National Football League, they have two representatives. A twenty-ninth member is a representative of the Pro Football Writers Association and the thirtieth is a "member-at-large."

Though the members of the Board of Selectors nominate and elect the members of the Hall of Fame, any *fan* may nominate someone simply by writing to the Hall of Fame. The only restriction is that a player must have been retired at least five years before he can be considered. For example, a candidate for the 1990 class must have finished his career not later than the 1984 season. For a nonplayer, there is no mandatory retirement period. However, a coach must be retired before he may be considered. Every nomination received by the Hall of Fame is processed and forwarded to the Board of Selectors.

The board meets annually at the time of the Super Bowl to elect new

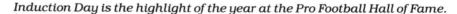

Induction Day is the highlight of the year at the Pro Football Hall of Fame.

Hall of Fame members. While there is no set number of new enshrinees, there is a rule that says that between four and seven new enshrinees will be elected each year. In order to be elected, a nominee must receive more than 80 percent approval from the board.

Every nomination is carefully considered. In order to assure that older players are not forgotten, a Senior Committee, made up of five veteran members of the board, nominates an "old-timer" candidate. His name is then placed on the final list. The other finalists consist of the survivors from the preliminary list of some sixty to seventy candidates that the board has screened through a mail-in vote.

It is important to emphasize that the Hall of Fame staff itself has no say as to who is or who isn't elected. The only function of the staff is to process the nominations received by the fans and to coordinate the annual meeting.

How are pro football teams named?

In the NFL's early years, it was common for a team to borrow the name of a major league baseball team from the same city. That's what the NFL's team from New York did in 1925. They took the name "Giants" from New York's National League baseball team. Using the name of a team's sponsor was also popular back then. The name "Packers" was a natural for the pro team located in Green Bay, Wisconsin, since the Indian Packing Company supplied the jerseys and practice field for the team.

Fan contests have produced the names of several NFL teams, including the Kansas City Chiefs, the Tampa Bay Buccaneers, the Seattle Seahawks, and the Cleveland Browns. The name "Browns" was adopted in recognition of the team's first coach, Paul Brown. When he was appointed, he was already an extremely popular figure in Ohio, having been a successful coach at Ohio State and Massillon High School. The name "Panthers" had been the winning entry in Cleveland's fan contest; however, after being reminded that there was once an unsuccessful pro team in Cleveland called the "Panthers," Brown vetoed the choice, claiming he didn't want anything to do with a team that "smacked of failure."

Other teams have chosen names that identify them with their community. In 1941, the NFL's Pittsburgh franchise changed its name from "Pirates," the name of the city's baseball team, to "Steelers" to represent the very important steel industry of the Pittsburgh area.

The Philadelphia Eagles, founded in 1933 during America's Great Depression, adopted the eagle, the symbol of the government's National Recovery Act, as their name and logo.

Of course, some team nicknames are less meaningful, such as the Phoenix Cardinals. The Cardinals, who originally played in Chicago, were not named after a majestic bird or a member of the Catholic clergy or the baseball team in St. Louis, where they played from 1960 to 1987. They took their name from the used "cardinal red" jerseys the team purchased from the University of Chicago. In fact, many early team names were derived from colors. The Chicago Cardinals' crosstown rivals, the Bears, were originally known as the Decatur "Staleys," because they were sponsored by the Staley Starch Works and played in Decatur, Illinois. When George Halas bought the team and moved them to Chicago, he renamed them the "Bears." His reasoning was that football players were bigger than baseball players, and since Chicago had the baseball "Cubs," his football team would be the "Bears."

Who was the first black man to play pro football?

Even though many blacks play in the National Football League today, it wasn't always that way. In fact, from 1920 to 1932, there were only thirteen black men in the NFL. From 1933 to 1945, there were none. Then, in 1946, Kenny Washington and Woodie Strode signed with the Los Angeles Rams and Bill Willis and Marion Motley signed with the Cleveland Browns. These four pioneers once again opened the doors of opportunity for blacks in pro football.

However, the first black man to play pro football played before Washington, Strode, Willis, or Motley were born. His name was Charles Follis. Known as the Black Cyclone, he played halfback for the Shelby, Ohio, Athletic Club in the pre-NFL years of 1902–6. Research suggests that he played as an amateur until 1904, and that it was big news in

At the right of the middle row sits Charles Follis of the Shelby Athletic Club, the first black man to play professional football.

30

Shelby when Follis signed his 1904 pro contract.

Though the fans in Shelby always supported Follis, there were cases of racial abuse in other cities the team visited. At a game in Toledo, Ohio, fans shouted racial insults at Follis. The Toledo team captain stopped play and shouted to the crowd to stop. The crowd applauded the Toledo captain's action and obeyed his request.

Considering the unfair hardships that Follis must have met, it would have been easy for him to simply quit. But he didn't. He continued to play until injury forced his retirement from football in 1906.

What is the record for the longest field goal?

The record stands at an amazing 63 yards. It was kicked by Tom Dempsey of the New Orleans Saints on November 8, 1970. It was one of the great moments in football history. Only eleven seconds remained when Errol Mann kicked an 18-yard field goal to put the Lions ahead of the Saints. But then the Saints' Al Dodd ran back the kickoff to their own 28-yard line. On the next play, he caught a pass and skipped out of bounds at the Saints' 45. With just two seconds to go, the Saints decided to try a 63-yard field goal. No one had ever kicked one that far.

"I knew I could kick it that far," Demp-

It has been two decades since Tom Dempsey set an NFL record with this 63-yard field goal, the culmination of one of the sport's most thrilling games.

sey said afterward, "but whether or not I could kick it straight that far kept running through my mind."

Dempsey, who was born with no toes on his right foot and with a right arm that ended in only two fingers, without a hand, had accepted challenges all his life. This was just another one. "There was pressure and I felt it," he said, "but I tried to shut it out of my mind."

The ball was snapped back to the holder. Dempsey swung his right leg forward, hitting it perfectly with his specially made square-toed shoe. At first, he said he couldn't see whether the kick cleared the crossbar. But when he saw the officials' arms go up and a big roar rose from the crowd, he knew it was good. The underdog Saints won the game, 19–17. "It was quite a thrill," Dempsey said afterward. "I'm still shook up."

What is the most famous play of all time?

Two great plays stand out in football history. The first is known as the "Immaculate Reception." It occurred on the final play of a 1972 American Football Conference playoff between the young Pittsburgh Steelers and the powerful Oakland Raiders.

With just twenty-two seconds remaining, the Steelers, who hadn't been in a playoff game since 1947, were trailing the Raiders, 7–6. Faced with a fourth-down situation at the Steelers' own 40-yard line, quarterback Terry Bradshaw dropped back to pass. His plan was to try and move the ball into field goal range. Bradshaw spotted running back Frenchy Fuqua streaking downfield and fired a pass in his direction. Just as the ball came within Fuqua's reach, it ricocheted off Raiders defense back Jack Tatum to the Steelers' other running back, Franco Harris, who bent forward and caught the ball at his shoetops. Without losing a step, Harris raced 42 yards for a touchdown. The Steelers won, 13–7. This victory marked the beginning of a decade of dominance by the Steelers, during which they won four Super Bowls.

The second famous play is referred to as the "Hail Mary" pass. It happened during the 1975 National Football Conference divisional playoff game between the Dallas Cowboys and the Minnesota Vikings.

Trailing the Vikings 14–10 with just thirty-two seconds remaining, the Cow-

Franco Harris of the Pittsburgh Steelers.

Roger Staubach of the Dallas Cowboys prepares to launch a bomb, like the "Hail Mary" pass he made famous in 1975.

boys needed a touchdown to win. "Our only hope," Dallas coach Tom Landry later remarked, "was to throw and hope for a miracle." So from the 50-yard line, Cowboys quarterback Roger Staubach did just that. Staubach's pass was short. However, wide receiver Drew Pearson saw what was happening and ran back for the short toss. "I reached back and caught it on my hip," he told reporters. With defenders all around him, he rolled into the end zone for the winning score. "I guess it's a 'Hail Mary' pass," Staubach stated. "You throw it up and pray he catches it."

Can you explain the difference between a placekick, a punt, and a dropkick?

Since the game begins with a placekick, let's start with that. Simply put, a placekick is when a ball is kicked from a fixed position on the ground or a kicking tee. The placekick is used to kick off after a score or to begin a half.

Lou Groza. Hall of Fame place kicker.

Also, the placekick is used for extra-point and field goal attempts.

On the kickoff, the ball is placed on a kicking tee. On some occasions, such as when a strong wind is blowing, a teammate is permitted to place his finger on the top point of the ball to keep it from blowing off the tee. This happens often in windy cities such as Chicago and Cleveland. For extra-point and field goal attempts, the ball is always held by a teammate and a tee is not permitted.

A punt is a kick made when a player drops a ball and kicks it before it hits the ground. Usually, a punt occurs on fourth down when a team doesn't feel it can gain a first down or is too far away to try a field goal. However, a team can punt the ball at any time. A punt on any down but fourth is usually intended to surprise the defense. When this happens, the punt is called a "quick kick." Since the defense is not expecting a punt, they are unprepared to return it and the ball usually rolls dead deep in their territory. A "quick kick" is usually kicked by a quarterback or running back. Denver Broncos quarterback John Elway has been known to try the "quick kick," as has Philadelphia Eagles quarterback Randall Cunningham.

A dropkick is made when a player drops a ball and kicks it just as it hits the ground. Originally, it was a preferred method to the placekick for field goal and extra-point attempts. The

Danny White of Dallas punts.

dropkick began to lose its popularity after a rule change in 1934 made the ball more pointed, taking almost an inch off its circumference. With the new thinner, sharp-pointed ball, dropkickers were not as able to get a good bounce.

Though the dropkick is still a legal kick, it hasn't been attempted in the NFL for many years. The last successful attempt occurred in the 1941 Championship Game. Leading the New York Giants, 36–9, Chicago Bear Scooter McLean dropkicked the game's final extra point for a joke. Not too many coaches would see the humor in that today, so don't look for another dropkick in the near future.

Jim Thorpe demonstrates the drop kick.

Who was Papa Bear?

George (Papa Bear) Halas was a pro football pioneer who was involved in the National Football League from its beginning in 1920 until his death in 1983. At one time or another, Halas filled the shoes of owner, general manager, player, promoter, rules maker, and coach. He even attended the NFL's organizational meeting in 1920, the same year he founded the Decatur Staleys football team. Never heard of the Staleys? Well, maybe this will help. A year later, he moved the Staleys to Chicago and in 1922 renamed the team the Chicago Bears.

Papa Bear Halas was more than just the founding father of the Chicago Bears, however. He was the team's star end, manager, and coach. Though he retired as a player in 1929, he con-

tinued to coach the Bears for forty years. Actually, his forty-year coaching career was divided into four packages. In 1929, when he retired as a player, he also "fired" himself as coach. However, in 1933, claiming he was the cheapest coach he could find, he rehired himself. When World War II broke out, his second coaching tenure was interrupted by a U.S. Navy assignment. He returned to coach for a third time in 1946, but retired again after ten seasons. In 1957, after a two-year break, he returned again for a final ten-year coaching tour. In 1968, Papa Bear, who was seventy-three years old, retired from coaching for good.

During his forty years as coach, Halas led the Bears to 325 victories, far more than any other pro coach. Under

his leadership, the Bears won six NFL championships and finished below the .500 mark just six times.

As a coach, he was a real innovator. He was the first to hold daily practice sessions and the first to extensively use game films for study. But, as any of his former players will tell you, he was also a strict disciplinarian. His word was law. If you didn't like the way he wanted it done, he wouldn't hesitate to tell you to do it somewhere else. Though tough on them, Halas took a personal interest in his players and their futures. "The qualities that make a winning player," he wrote in his autobiography, *Halas by Halas*, "bring successes throughout life." And many former Bears did find success after football. "Of the nineteen league players who became physicians or surgeons," Papa Bear bragged, "nine are Bears."

George "Papa Bear" Halas with one of his favorite cubs, Hall of Fame quarterback Sid Luckman.

Do players have to wear certain numbers on their jerseys?

In 1973, a jersey-numbering system was adopted by the National Football League. The system provides that numbers 1–19 are reserved for quarterbacks and specialists; 20–49 for running backs and defensive backs; 50–59 for centers and linebackers; 60–79 for defensive linemen and interior offensive linemen other than centers; and 80–89 for wide receivers and tight ends. Numbers in the 90s were not des- ignated for defensive ends, but that is the way things have worked out.

When the rule was made, it was also decided that players in the NFL in 1972 could continue to use their old numbers.

This was not the first numbering system adopted by the league. In 1952, when single-platoon football was beginning to die out, the *NFL Rules Book* stated that players must be numbered

Otto Graham's Cleveland Browns number changed from 60 to 14, but his jersey stayed the same.

according to their positions. Centers were to wear numbers 50–59; guards 60–69; tackles 70–79; ends 80–89; halfbacks 20–29 and 40–49; fullbacks 30–39, and quarterbacks 13–19. The rule had one exception. "Nationally known players" who had been in the league for three or more years were allowed to keep their old numbers, but by 1953 most players had changed to the new system.

An interesting object on display at the Hall of Fame is Otto Graham's 1953 Cleveland Browns jersey. Graham, the great Hall of Fame quarterback, changed his number from 60 to 14. Rather than give him a new jersey, however, the Browns' equipment man simply peeled off his old number and sewed on the new one. Along with the several stitched repairs, you can still see the outline of the number 60 under the 14.

Have more than two brothers ever played on the same NFL team?

Though it was common for brothers to play on the same team in the pre-NFL years, it's happened only twice in the NFL. The first team to include more than two brothers was the 1920 Columbus Panhandles. Actually, the pre-NFL Panhandles had for many years featured six brothers: Al, Phil, Ted, John, Frank, and Fred Nesser. In 1920, when the team joined the NFL, only three of the famous brothers—Frank, Phil, and Ted—were still on the roster. However, brothers John and Fred rejoined the team for the 1921 season.

Pro football's fab five—the Nesser brothers.

Brother Al was happy playing with the Akron Pros and did not return to join his brothers. Unbelievable as it may sound, a seventh brother, Raymond, and Ted's son, Charles, joined the family act for at least a few games that season.

The next and only other time more than two brothers played on the same NFL team occurred in 1924 when Joe, Cobb, and Bill Rooney suited up for the Duluth, Minnesota, Kelleys. After a few games in 1925, brother Bill's contract was sold to the New York Giants for $100. However, the three were reunited in 1927 when they played for the same Duluth team, which was renamed the Duluth Eskimos.

Though there have been other cases of three or more brothers playing in the NFL—such as, in recent years, Joey, Ross, Jim, and Keith Browner—no more than two have played for the same team during the same season since the Rooney brothers.

What was the greatest come-from-behind win a team ever made?

If your team was up 28 points at halftime, you'd probably feel that you had the game won. Right? Well, I'll bet the New Orleans Saints felt that way on December 7, 1980. They were leading the San Francisco 49ers 35–7 at halftime. And, after all, this was the same 49ers that won just two games the year before. However, it was also the same 49ers who would win the Super Bowl the next year.

Anyway, San Francisco, behind the passing of Joe Montana and the running of Lenvil Elliott, staged a record comeback by scoring 28 points in the second half to tie the score 35–35. In overtime, Ray Wersching kicked a 36-yard field goal, giving the 49ers the win.

You can imagine how disappointed the Saints and their fans must have been. In the first half, the Saints out-gained the 49ers 324 yards to just 21. They set team records of 376 yards passing and 519 yards in total offense. But still they lost. This just wasn't their game. Actually, 1980 just wasn't the Saints' year. Their final record was a dismal 1–15.

What was the greatest pro football game ever played?

In his book, *NFL Top 40*, Shelby Strother wrote: "Selecting pro football's Top 40 games is about as easy as picking up soap bubbles with chopsticks." So just imagine how difficult it is to pick just one.

First of all, if by "greatest" we just mean entertaining, then dozens of games could be considered. However, for a game to be called the "greatest," it should be significant in a special way, as well as entertaining.

The Baltimore Colts' Alan Ameche rips through the line of the New York Giants in the historic 1958 Championship Game.

Only fifty cents then, but a treasured memento today—the program of what many have called "the greatest game ever played."

And so we arrive at three choices: the 1932 indoor game between the Chicago Bears and the Portsmouth Spartans; Super Bowl III between the New York Jets and the Baltimore Colts; and the 1958 National Football League Championship Game between the Baltimore Colts and the New York Giants.

The 1932 indoor game is not only responsible for the start of postseason playoffs, but also for some very important rule changes, including legalizing the forward pass from anywhere behind the line of scrimmage and the use of inbound hash marks. Both rules helped to open up offenses and increase the popularity of the sport.

In Super Bowl III, between the New York Jets and the Baltimore Colts, Jets quarterback Joe Namath "guaranteed" a victory. Huge underdogs, the Jets represented the young American Football League, while the Colts represented the older NFL. Both the Jets and the AFL were considered by many to be inferior in terms of the quality of play. So when they beat the Colts, 16–7, it proved that both the Jets and the AFL were equal to the task. The amazing upset also did much to popularize the Super Bowl series.

The third game, the 1958 NFL Championship Game between the Baltimore Colts and the New York Giants, is often referred to as "the greatest game ever played." It was an overtime classic that ended with a 1-yard touchdown dive by fullback Alan Ameche that gave the Colts a remarkable 23–17 win.

The game was full of surprises and heroes. Colts quarterback Johnny Unitas was named the game's MVP. With five minutes left in regulation play, everyone expected the award would go to Giants quarterback Charlie Conerly. But, with 1:56 remaining and down, 17–14, Unitas marched the Colts downfield. Three straight Unitas passes to Raymond Berry, gaining 62 yards, highlighted the drive. With seven seconds left, Colts placekicker Steve Myhra kicked a 20-yard field goal to send the game into overtime.

Having won the coin toss, the Giants got the ball first. Unable to gain a first down, they punted. The Giants never got another chance. Unitas and the Colts ran thirteen plays for 80 yards and the win.

The game was not only exciting but

was the first sudden-death Championship Game ever played. Making it all the more significant was the fact that it was nationally televised. Many feel the game marked the beginning of pro football's greatest period of growth in popularity.

If you'd like to know more about great games, read *NFL Top 40* by Shelby Strother. If you'd like to read a detailed account of the 1958 Championship Game, check out John Steadman's *The Greatest Football Game Ever Played.*

Do pro football players have to wear helmets?

Modern football rules require players to wear helmets. But that wasn't always the case. In the early days of pro football, players had a choice. Some thought it more manly to go without. That was during the days when football was mostly a pushing-and-shoving game. As you know, the game has changed over the years. Players have gotten bigger and stronger and rule changes have made the game a faster, harder-hitting sport.

Still, the National Football League didn't require a player to wear a helmet until 1943. By then, the majority of players were wearing them by choice.

The Chicago Bears' Bill Hewitt was one of the last men to play in the NFL without a helmet. Here he laterals to Bill Karr for the winning touchdown in the 1933 title game against the New York Giants.

41

Can you find Bill Hewitt in this 1937 picture?

Dick Plasman of the Chicago Bears is believed to be the last player to play without a helmet. Photos of him in the 1940 NFL Championship Game show that he didn't wear one. Hall of Famer Bill Hewitt, another former Bear, played without a helmet right up until he retired in 1939. In 1943, he came back for one season, but by then the league rule required him to wear a helmet.

Helmets are perhaps the most important piece of equipment worn by a player today. As a result, before a helmet is approved for use by the NFL, it must pass several safety standards.

What was the "Ice Bowl"?

Even the most dedicated football fan would have to think twice about sitting through a game like the "Ice Bowl." The 1967 National Football League Championship Game between the Green Bay Packers and the Dallas Cowboys was given the nickname because the weather was so cold—a frigid thirteen degrees below zero at game time. Packer fans have always been known as a hardy bunch. But thirteen below zero? Nonetheless, more than fifty thousand fans packed Green Bay's Lambeau Field that New Year's Eve day to see their Packers play for a third straight NFL crown.

From the start, Green Bay fans felt their team had an edge in this game.

The Packers were more familiar with the cold Green Bay weather conditions. They lived and practiced in those conditions. And the fact that they jumped out to a 14–0 lead in the second quarter probably convinced the fans that they were right. However, the bone-chilling cold affected even the Packers. Dallas scored a touchdown and a field goal after two Packer fumbles and added a second TD in the fourth quarter. Suddenly, with 4:50 left in the game, the Packers were behind, 17–14.

Cold or not, the Packers didn't give up. Behind the leadership of Hall of Fame quarterback Bart Starr, they marched downfield. With sixteen seconds remaining and the temperature down to eighteen below zero, the Packers were about two feet away from victory. Starr called timeout. The field was like a sheet of ice. The two previous running plays had gone nowhere. With no timeouts left, a running play seemed totally out of the question. A completed pass would surely win it. Even an incomplete pass would at least stop the clock so the Packers could set up a field goal to tie the game and send it into overtime. After consulting with Packers coach Vince Lombardi, Starr returned to the huddle. "Which pass play will it be?" the frozen Packer fans wondered.

Starr took the center snap from Ken Bowman. Bowman and guard Jerry Kramer combined to take out Dallas tackle Jethro Pugh. With Pugh out of the way, Starr surprised everyone and dove over for the score. "We had run out of ideas," Starr later said of the play. However, coach Lombardi put it another way, "We gambled and we won."

What was the most lopsided game ever played?

The most one-sided game in pro-football history was certainly the 1940 NFL Championship Game, when the Chicago Bears beat the Washington Redskins, 73–0. A real blowout!

While no team should ever have trouble getting motivated for a Championship Game, the Bears were really eager to play this one. Their pride was as much at stake as the league championship. Three weeks earlier the Redskins had defeated the Bears, 7–3. In that game, the Bears complained about the officiating. They claimed the Redskins should have been called for pass interference on the game's final play, a 6-yard pass into the end zone which, had it been completed, would have

The Bears' George McAfee goes up and over the line in the famous 73-0 rout of the Washington Redskins in the 1940 Championship Game.

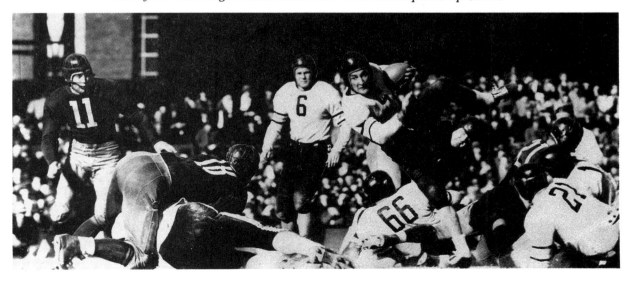

Washington's Griffith Stadium, scene of the crime.

given the Bears the win. But the game official disagreed. Redskins owner George Marshall foolishly got in the act by calling the Bears "crybabies," "quitters," and "a first-half team." As you can imagine, this only angered the Bears more. They couldn't wait for their chance to get even.

According to former Bears fullback Bill Osmanski, "They almost broke the locker room door down getting out to the field" on the day of the Championship Game. It was Osmanski who scored first. He bolted 68 yards for a touchdown on the game's second play. The Bears scored three more touchdowns and led, 28–0, at the half.

In the locker room at halftime, coach George Halas reminded the Bears of Marshall's remarks, including the charge that the Bears were "a first-half

team." Halas's words weren't wasted. The Bears scored 26 points in the third quarter and 19 more in the fourth.

Ten different players scored touchdowns. Five different players kicked extra points. After the tenth touchdown, referee Red Friesel instructed the Bears to either pass or run for the extra point. It seems that the refs were running low on footballs. Every time an extra point was kicked, a ball had been lost to the fans in the end zone seats. So, adding insult to the Redskins' injury, backup quarterback Sollie Sherman passed successfully for the extra point. The Bears scored yet another touchdown, to exact their revenge against the hapless Redskins, thus reaching the final score of 73–0, providing pro football with its most lopsided game.

What are some of the best nicknames for offensive and defensive squads?

Football has always been a great sport for nicknames. Not only do players have great nicknames, such as Too Tall Jones or William (the Refrigerator) Perry, but entire offensive and defensive squads have them as well. Let's take a look at a few.

In the 1960s, the Los Angeles Rams' defensive front terrorized their opponents with their speed and strength.

That unit became known as the Fearsome Foursome. It included two Hall of Famers, Merlin Olsen and Deacon Jones. Jones, often called the Secretary of Defense by the press, is the man who came up with the term "sack" when referring to tackling the quarterback. Olsen went on to star in several popular television shows, including "Father Murphy" and "Aaron's Way."

Another defensive unit with a great nickname was the Minnesota Vikings' Purple People Eaters. This group of defensive stars played in the late 1960s and 1970s. Hall of Famer Alan Page, the first lineman ever to be named Most Valuable Player in the NFL, was a longtime member. In 1970 alone, the Purple People Eaters had 49 quarterback sacks for a total of 360 lost yards.

Perhaps the best-known defensive unit of the 1970s was the Pittsburgh Steelers' Steel Curtain. This defensive "curtain" was anchored by Hall of Fame tackle Joe Greene, whose own nickname was Mean Joe.

The Steel Curtain had perhaps its finest year in 1976. In the final nine games of that season, it held opponents to just 28 points. It shut out the opposition five times and gave up only two touchdowns.

The first offensive line to gain fame as a group and earn a nickname was the Buffalo Bills' Electric Company. Just as an electric company turns on the electrical "juice," the Bills' Electric Company turned on the Juice, the Bills' great running back and Hall of Famer O. J. Simpson.

There have been other nicknames, such as Dallas's Doomsday Defense or

The Fearsome Foursome: Merlin Olsen (74), Lamar Lundy (partially hidden), Deacon Jones (75), and Roger Brown (78).

Pittsburgh's Steel Curtain in action against the Cleveland Browns.

Denver's Orange Crush, but one of the best belongs to the Washington Redskins' offensive linemen, called the Hogs. The Hogs were nicknamed in 1981, when coach Joe Bugel assembled the biggest and strongest offensive line he could find. They *averaged* six-five and 280 pounds. One day Bugel, when calling his men to practice, said, "Okay, you hogs, let's go."

"Some guys might have resented it," Bugel said later, "but these guys loved it." Not only did the players love it, but the fans and the press did too. Suddenly, the Redskins' offensive linemen—the guys who are usually overlooked by the fans and press—were famous. And all because of a not-so-glamorous nickname, the Hogs.

When was the first pro football game played at night?

Pro football's first night game was played way back on November 21, 1902, at Elmira, New York. The Philadelphia Athletics beat the Kanaweola Athletic Club, 39–0. The field was surrounded with ground-level floodlights and "glaring searchlights" behind the goal posts. Supposedly, the lights in the end zones were almost blinding to the players, making it difficult to see the goal lines. From the looks of the score, the A's must have worn their sunglasses.

The first night game played in the National Football League occurred several years later on November 6, 1929, in Providence, Rhode Island's Kinsley Park. There the Chicago Cardinals defeated the Providence Steam Roller, 16–0. Unlike the Elmira game, Kinsley Park was well lit. The local newspaper wrote that "two rows of monster floodlights brought out the team colors with theatrical brightness." To help players spot the ball in the dark, it was painted white. According to the same newspaper, the ball looked like "a large egg." Though the hometown Steam Roller lost the game, the only complaint mentioned by the newspaper was that "an illuminated scoreboard would have helped." You can't please *everyone!*

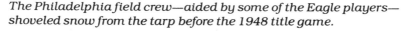

Has a football game ever been canceled due to rain or snow?

In pro football's early years, games were canceled on many occasions due to rain. There may have been one that was canceled by snow, but no one today knows of it.

Rain cancellations, while fairly common, weren't because players were opposed to playing, but rather because fans wouldn't attend. There were no TV or radio contracts back then. Game

The Philadelphia field crew—aided by some of the Eagle players—shoveled snow from the tarp before the 1948 title game.

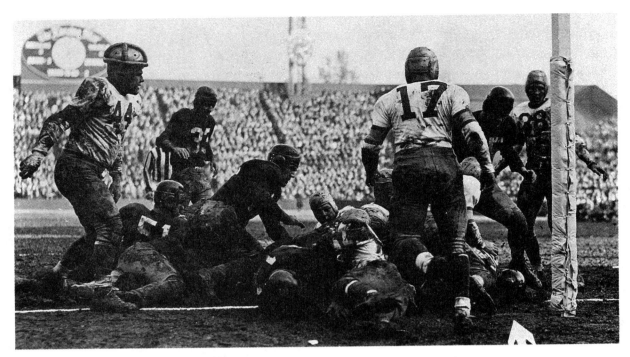

Even big boys sometimes like to play in the mud.

admissions were just about the only source of income a team had and home teams had to pay a guaranteed amount to a visiting team. If the attendance was low, the home team had a hard time paying the bills. It just made more sense to cancel the game.

One typical game contract from 1929 stated that the home team had the right to cancel the game due to "inclement weather." However, they had to do so at least five hours before the visiting team's train was scheduled to depart.

In more recent times, two exhibition games were forced to end early because of rain. The first was the 1976 College All-Star Game between the Pittsburgh Steelers and the College All-Stars. Played at Chicago's Soldier Field, the game was called with 1:22 remaining in the third quarter, after heavy thundershowers flooded the playing field.

The other early finish due to rain was the 1980 Hall of Fame Game be-

tween the San Diego Chargers and the Green Bay Packers. A severe storm accompanied by lightning ended this game with 5:29 remaining in the fourth quarter.

In 1961, a game was canceled due to a hurricane warning. The Boston Patriots of the old American Football League were scheduled to play the Buffalo Bills on a Friday night at Boston University Stadium. According to Larry Fox in his book *The New England Patriots: Triumph and Tragedy*, there were "warnings of both a hurricane and a small crowd that night." So the Patriots, fearing both, asked league permission to delay the game until Sunday. The hurricane never appeared, but neither did many fans.

The Bills lost the game, 52–21, and Buffalo head coach Buster Ramsey was understandably upset. The team had arrived in Boston on Thursday expecting to play on Friday. Instead, they were forced to stay an additional two days in a motel waiting for a storm that never showed up. As Fox points out in his book, "Few players carried more than a toothbrush, a razor, and one change of linens, if that, on those short trips." Personally, I think I would have rather faced the hurricane than the Bills' fiery coach.

When a quarterback is tackled, why is it called a "sack"?

When a quarterback is tackled behind the line of scrimmage, it's described as a "sack," thanks to one of the greatest "sackers" of all time, Deacon Jones.

Jones, a former star defensive end with the Los Angeles Rams, felt that it took up too much room in headlines to say that a player "tackled the quarterback behind the line of scrimmage."

"We needed a shorter term," he said. He gave it some thought and came up with the term "sack." He said he liked the term, "because, like, you know, you sack a city—you devastate it." And that is just what Deacon Jones did for fourteen seasons. He sacked quarterbacks and devastated offenses.

Deacon really liked nicknames. They

David "Deacon" Jones, 1980 Hall of Fame enshrinee and sacker supreme.

49

seemed to follow him throughout his career. In fact, his real first name is David. When he was a rookie, he was afraid no one would remember a player with a common name like David Jones, so he gave himself the nickname Deacon. The press nicknamed him the Secretary of Defense of his defensive line, the Fearsome Foursome.

But by any name, Deacon Jones was one of the best. And in 1980 the man who was the "master sacker" was elected to the Hall of Fame.

Who invented the shotgun formation?

The shotgun formation was popularized back in 1960 by San Francisco 49ers head coach Red Hickey. He first used the formation on November 27 of that year in a game against the Baltimore Colts.

Hickey knew the Colts had a terrific pass rush. He thought if he moved his quarterback seven yards behind the center, it would give him more time to spot his receivers. Also, he hoped the new-looking formation would force the

John Brodie of the 49ers, riding shotgun.

Colts to change their defense. He was right on both accounts. The 49ers defeated the Colts, 30–22. Using the shotgun formation, the 49ers won three of the four remaining games of the 1960 season and quarterback John Brodie became known as "the man who pulled the trigger of the shotgun."

In 1961, Brodie and the 49ers found the formation's magic still alive. Their quick 4–1 start included back-to-back 49–0 and 35–0 wins over the Detroit Lions and the Los Angeles Rams. However, in a game against the Chicago Bears on October 22, the shotgun misfired. Bears linebacker and Hall of Famer Bill George found a weakness. Instead of lining up in his usual linebacker spot, George moved up to the line of scimmage. With his added presence, the Bears were able to penetrate by attacking the center and getting

through to Brodie. After harassing the 49ers' quarterback all afternoon, the Bears clobbered San Francisco, 31–0.

Soon after that game, Hickey figured his shotgun was dead and retired the play. However, several years later, the formation returned when Tom Landry and the Dallas Cowboys added it to their offensive strategy. With the adjustments made by Landry and the Cowboys, the play again became a powerful weapon. Today just about every NFL team includes the shotgun formation in its playbook, particularly for third-and-long situations. The pro defenses, however, have adjusted to the shotgun by bringing in a fifth, or "nickel," defensive back for third-and-long situations.

And so it goes: for every offensive innovation, opposing teams come up with a defensive solution.

What were the strangest uniforms?

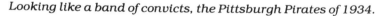

The uniforms worn by the National Football League's 1934 Pittsburgh Pirates are probably the most ridiculous-

looking uniforms ever seen on a pro football field. The horizontally striped black-and-gold jerseys with matching

Looking like a band of convicts, the Pittsburgh Pirates of 1934.

socks made the players look more like prison convicts then football players. They were "pretty bad," according to former player Armand Niccolai. "But since we had to buy our own shoes, helmets, and pads, we were just thankful to have uniforms." The uniforms didn't last long. They were dumped after one season.

What is a "wild card" team and how does the NFL's playoff system work?

The answer to this question gets a little complicated. First, as you probably already know, there are two conferences in the National Football League: the American Football Conference (AFC) and the National Football Conference (NFC). In each conference there are three divisions—the Eastern, Western, and Central. Each division has a champion. This means there are three division champions in the AFC and three in the NFC. Then there are two "wild card" teams in each conference. They are the two best second-place teams in each conference.

The playoffs begin with the wild card teams from the same conference playing each other. The winners advance to the divisional playoff games. Here the winning wild card team plays the division champion in its conference with the best regular season record. The two remaining division champions in each conference play each other.

There is one exception to this system. If the winner of the wild card game and the division champion with the best regular season record are from the same division, they *don't* play each other. Instead, the wild card team plays the division champion with the *second-best* regular season record, and the remaining division champions play each other.

The next round is called the Conference Championship Games. Here the winners of the divisional playoff games meet. The winners from the AFC play each other and the winners from the NFC play each other. The result is one AFC champion and one NFC champion. Finally, these two teams meet in the Super Bowl. Clear? Well, perhaps the chart below will help.

First-Round Playoff Games
AFC Wild Card vs. AFC Wild Card
NFC Wild Card vs. NFC Wild Card
Divisional Playoff Games
Winning AFC Wild Card vs. AFC Div. Champ. with the best record
AFC Div. Champ. with 2nd-best record vs. AFC Div. Champ. with 3rd-best record
Winning NFC Wild Card vs. NFC Div. Champ. with the best record
NFC Div. Champ. with 2nd-best record vs. NFC Div. Champ. with 3rd-best record
Conference Championship Games
Winner of 1st AFC Div. Playoff Game vs. Winner of 2nd AFC Div. Playoff Game
Winner of 1st NFC Div. Playoff Game vs. Winner of 2nd NFC Div. Playoff Game
Super Bowl Game
Winner of AFC Champ. Game vs. Winner of NFC Champ. Game

What was the first team
to use the team logo on the team's helmets?

The first team to have a helmet logo was the Los Angeles Rams. They started the trend way back in 1947, when Rams halfback Fred Gehrke, who in the offseason was a designer for an aircraft company, was asked to design a new uniform for the team. The helmet logo—ram's horns—was part of the design he came up with.

The logo was an immediate hit. The only problem was that the Rams couldn't find a way to stencil it on to the seventy leather helmets they had on hand. So head coach Bob Snyder

Fred Gehrke (left), designer of the Rams' logo helmet, poses with Rams' rookie running back Glenn Davis before a 1948 preseason game.

instructed Gehrke to hand paint each one. Throughout the summer, Gehrke worked evenings and weekends until he completed the job. Unfortunately, the task didn't end when the seventy helmets were finished. Throughout the 1948 season, whenever a helmet chipped or cracked, Gehrke was called on for a quick touch-up.

In 1949, the Rams decided to purchase new plastic helmets to replace the old leather ones. Fortunately, the helmet manufacturer was able to apply the logo to the helmets through a special painting process. Happily, Fred Gehrke's helmet-painting career was over. Unfortunately, however, after 1949 Gehrke's Ram career was over too.

Which National Football League team doesn't have a logo on its helmet? There's only one, the Cleveland Browns, because the Browns don't have an official logo.

What is the "two-minute warning"?

One of the responsibilities of the game referee is to notify head coaches when only two minutes of playing time remain in either half. This is referred to as the "two-minute warning." It is an automatic officials' timeout. On a strategic level, it signals the beginning of a period in which the trailing team, if it has the ball, relies on the sideline pass and the wide run. This is because the clock stops on an incomplete pass or run that ends out of bounds. If the trailing team is on defense, it will use up its remaining timeouts in an effort to regain possession with some time still left to mount an attack.

Teams used to try all sorts of maneuvers to conserve time or stop the clock at the end of a game. Often, players would fake injuries. Special rules were developed to discourage such behavior. For example, the kickoff rule is different during the last two minutes of the halves. During the rest of the game, the clock starts when the ball is kicked. In the two-minute period, the clock doesn't start until a member of the receiving team touches the ball. Another difference is that during the two-minute period, teams are charged for an injury timeout. During the rest of the game, an injury timeout is an officials' timeout.

So when the referee gives the "two-minute warning," he is alerting the coaches that these rules are in effect.

What is pro football's "Triple Crown"?

When a player wins three individual statistical championships in one year, it is said that he has won the "Triple Crown." Only three players—Sammy Baugh of the Washington Redskins, Steve Van Buren of the Philadelphia Eagles, and Bill Dudley of the Pittsburgh Steelers—have accomplished this rare feat. Also, all three managed to do it during a four-season period

Sammy Baugh of the Redskins.

The Eagles' Steve Van Buren.

Bill Dudley of the Steelers.

from 1943 to 1946. That may seem strange, but remember, players used to play both offense and defense. Some of the greatest offensive stars were also great on defense. This means the players back then had more opportunity to lead in different categories than today's specialist players. It also means that it is unlikely any other players will join Baugh, Van Buren, and Dudley on the list of Triple Crown winners.

The first to win the crown was Sammy Baugh. One of the greatest quarterbacks ever, Baugh was also an outstanding defensive player and punter. He won the Triple Crown in 1943 when he led the league in passing (133 attempts for 1754 yards), punting (45.9 yard average), and interceptions (11). Steve Van Buren followed in 1945 when he led in rushing (832 yards), scoring (110 points), and kickoff returns (13 for 373 yards and a 28.7 yard average). The final "Triple Crown" winner was Bill Dudley, who in 1946 led the league in rushing (604 yards), punt returns (27 for 385 yards and 14.2 average), and interceptions (10).

Another honor all three of these outstanding players won was election to the Pro Football Hall of Fame.

Why does a touchdown count for 6 points and a field goal 3 points?

The answer to this question goes all the way back to the 1860s, before pro football had even been born. Back then, the game was played by boys in high schools and some colleges. Score was kept by adding the number of goals scored in a game. Most scoring was done by kicking.

Then in 1883, a new point system was introduced. Touchdowns counted 2, a goal following a touchdown 4, and field goals 5 points. Two months later, a rules committee changed a touchdown's value to 4 points and the goal after a touchdown to 2. Field goals remained 5 points. That's the way it stood in 1892, when pro football played its first game. Five years later, in 1897, a touchdown was increased to 5 points

and the goal after reduced to 1. Again, the value of a field goal remained 5 points. Finally, in 1912, the value of a touchdown was changed to 6 points, the goal after, or point after, stayed at 1, and a field goal was reduced to 3. That is how it has remained since, with the exception of the American Football League's optional 2-point conversion in the 1960s.

The primary reason for the changes in scoring is that football, like its ancestors soccer and rugby, was originally mostly a kicking game. As the American game grew, it developed its own style and rules. Less emphasis was placed on the importance of kicking. As a result, nonkicking scoring plays were given a greater point value.

What was the "taxi squad"?

The term "taxi squad" originated with the Cleveland Browns in the late 1940s. The Browns' owner, Art McBride, owned a taxicab company. Rather than risk losing some of the players cut to meet his team's thirty-three-man roster, he gave them jobs with his cab company. If, during the course of the season, he needed to replace a player for any reason, he had an instant list to choose from—his taxi drivers!

Today the NFL uses a system that works much the same way as the "taxi squad" did. Those players who—for reasons of injury, military service, or other circumstances—are not immediately available for participation with a team are said to be on the reserve list. However, these players must meet the necessary requirements to be on the limited list and are restricted as to how and when they can be reactivated.

Has a player from a losing team ever been named Super Bowl MVP?

Even though Dallas Cowboys linebacker Chuck Howley made two key interceptions in Super Bowl V, it wasn't enough to stop the Baltimore Colts. Jim O'Brien's 32-yard field goal with just five seconds remaining gave the Colts a 16–13 victory. However, Howley's outstanding performance that day didn't go unrecognized. His team lost, but he was named the game's Most Valuable Player.

Not only is Howley the only player from a losing team to have won Super Bowl MVP honors, but he was also the first defensive player to receive the award.

Chuck Howley (54) of the Cowboys, MVP of Super Bowl V.

What is an onside kick and why would a team try it?

An onside kick is really just a short kickoff. It usually occurs late in the game when the kicking team is trailing. Rather than risk letting the receiving team have the ball again, the kicking team tries to take advantage of the rules. The rules say that a kickoff must only travel 10 yards and that the ball may be recovered by either team. So if the kicking team can recover the ball, it gives the team another chance to score before time runs out. If the kickoff is deep, the receiving team might run out the clock—or, worse yet, score again.

When attempting an onside kick, the kicker intentionally kicks the ball to one side of the field just beyond the required 10-yard distance. Immediately, the kicking team rushes forward and attempts to recover the ball. If they recover, they are almost certain to have good field position. Usually the kicker tries to kick it on the ground, making it difficult for the receiving team to handle. However, the receiving team in this situation is usually stocked with "good hands people"—backs and receivers—rather than linemen; fumbles are rare.

However, there are several risks involved in using the onside kick. First, if the kicking team doesn't recover, the receiving team will be very near scoring range. Second, if the ball doesn't travel the minimum distance, the kicking team is penalized 5 yards and must kick again. Finally, if the onside kick is kicked out of bounds, there is also a 5-yard penalty. If the ball is kicked out of bounds a second time, it is turned over to the receiving team at the yard line where it went out of bounds.

Who were the youngest and oldest players in NFL history?

As a twenty-year-old rookie in 1936, Dan Fortmann, a former Chicago Bears guard and Hall of Famer, is thought to have been the youngest player in NFL history.

Drafted in the last round out of Colgate, many thought Fortmann was too small at six feet and 207 pounds for NFL line play. He quickly proved his critics wrong. Named to the All-NFL team in six straight years, 1938–43, Fortmann was a deadly tackler on defense and a devastating blocker on offense. With Fortmann as the lead blocker, the Bears led the league in rushing four times. On defense, with Fort-mann in the lineup, the Bears held opponents to the fewest yards rushing in a season three times.

A smart player, Fortmann continued his studies while playing pro football and earned a medical degree that enabled him to become a practicing physician *before* retiring after the 1943 season. Fortmann later became the team doctor for the Los Angeles Rams.

The oldest player in NFL history was quarterback-kicker George Blanda, who played for the Bears, the Baltimore Colts, the Houston Oilers, and the Oakland Raiders. Blanda played for a total of twenty-six seasons before retiring in

Dan Fortmann, an NFLer at age twenty.

George Blanda, an NFLer at age forty-eight.

August of 1976, just weeks before his forty-ninth birthday.

In fact, Blanda first retired after the 1958 season when the Bears indicated they were going to use him strictly as a kicker. However, in 1960 he came out of retirement as the quarterback-kicker for the Houston Oilers of the new American Football League. He led the Oilers to two AFL championships and earned AFL Player of the Year honors for himself in 1961.

Though he holds several NFL records, including an amazing 2,002 ca-reer points, Blanda is best remembered for a string of last-minute heroics during the 1970 season as a member of the Oakland Raiders. In a five-game period, he provided the Raiders with four wins and a tie with last-second touchdown passes or field goals. While winning games for the Raiders, the ageless Blanda also won the hearts and admiration of many older NFL fans and became a national folk hero. In 1981, he won election to the Pro Football Hall of Fame.

Who was the greatest pass receiver?

Don Hutson of the Green Bay Packers was perhaps the greatest pass receiver ever to play pro football. Though it's been more than forty years since he played, his name still fills the *NFL Record Book*.

There are many things about Hutson that make him deserving of the title of "greatest." He was truly a man ahead of his time. He made pass receiving an art. His great speed and clever moves made him nearly impossible for defenders to cover. In a day when double coverage was rare, defenses frequently triple-teamed Hutson. On his very first play as a pro, he caught an 83-yard touchdown pass against the Chicago Bears. This was just the first of 99 touchdown receptions he would make in his career—still an NFL record. In his eleven-year career (1935–45), he led the league in receiving a record eight times. He also led the NFL in scoring for a record five consecutive years. And when he retired, Hutson led all receivers with 488 career receptions. The second-leading receiver as of that year trailed Don by an incredible 298 catches.

Hutson's finest season was 1942, when he caught an amazing 74 passes for 1,211 yards. This was the first time a receiver ever gained more than 1,000 yards in a season. In one game alone, he caught 14 passes. In addition, his 17 touchdowns and 138 points that year were both NFL records.

Like all players back then, Hutson played on defense as well as offense. As a defensive back, his sure hands served him well, catching dozens of opposing quarterbacks' passes. For several years, the Packers also relied on his talents as a placekicker.

As Don Smith points out in his book *Pro Football Hall of Fame All-Time Greats*, had it not been for a unique

Others may have caught more passes, but Don Hutson remains the greatest.

decision made by NFL president Joe Carr in 1935, Hutson might never have become a record-setting receiver. Coming out of college, Hutson signed contracts with two NFL teams: the Packers, a team that frequently went to the air, and the Brooklyn Dodgers, who rarely passed the ball. Carr ruled that the team that had mailed its contract first would be awarded the rights to Hutson. The Packers' contract had been postmarked at 8:30 A.M., while the Dodgers' came in at 8:47 A.M. the same day. So by a mere seventeen minutes, Don Hutson was a Packer.

What was the "flying wedge" play?

The "flying wedge" was a dangerous play used in the late 1890s and early 1900s. There is a good explanation of it

in a book in the Hall of Fame library titled *Foot-Ball*, written in 1892 by Carl Johanson, which tells how the play was designed by a Boston businessman and fan named Lorin Deland. Deland never played or coached football. However, he did play checkers. Using eleven red checkers against eleven black checkers, Deland made move after move until he perfected the "flying wedge."

It worked like this. After fielding a kickoff, the return man would stay behind his blockers, who would run downfield in a V-shaped formation. The V would run directly at the oncoming defense. At the last minute, just before contact, one side of the V would sweep forward, making a single slanted wall of interference. Sometimes the players would lock arms or hold straps sewn on their teammates' pants to keep the wall, or wedge, from being broken. It was a very dangerous play.

The idea of a wedge was not new. A "shoving wedge," designed to push an opposing line back from the line of scrimmage, had been used before. What the "flying wedge" added was a running start. This addition caused many serious injuries and even some deaths. It got so bad that, after the 1905 season ended, President Theodore Roosevelt called representatives from the major colleges to the White House. He warned them to "clean up football." As a result, several important changes in the rules were made, including the banning of the "flying

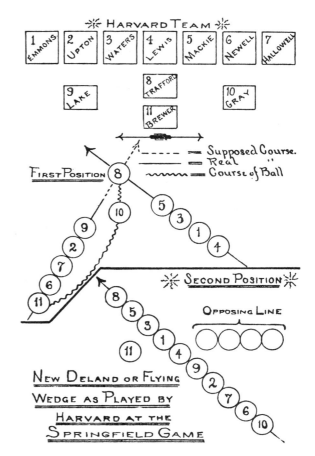

The "flying wedge" of 1892 was also called the "Deland," named for its inventor.

wedge." The new rules stated that seven men had to play on the line of scrimmage when the ball was snapped by the center. This resulted in the development of the "T formation."

Which team has the most enshrinees in the Pro Football Hall of Fame?

There are 148 individuals enshrined in the Hall of Fame. While some, like Roger Staubach of the Dallas Cowboys, spent their entire career with just one team, most did not. For instance, George Blanda played for four teams, the Chicago Bears (1949–58), the Baltimore Colts (1950), the Houston Oilers (1960–66), and the Oakland Raiders (1967–75), making significant contributions to the Bears, the Oilers, and the Raiders.

The Bears have sent the most players to the Hall of Fame: this 1940 squad alone sent six (George Musso, Bulldog Turner, Dan Fortmann, Joe Stydahar, George McAfee, and Sid Luckman).

Twenty-one different enshrinees are listed with the Chicago Bears as their primary team. This is the most for any team. Some, like Dick Butkus, played their entire career for the Bears. Others, like Mike Ditka, played a major portion of their careers with Chicago and therefore are listed as Bears. With eighteen enshrinees, the Green Bay Packers are second. It really shouldn't come as a surprise that the Bears and the Packers are so well represented. After all, the Bears have been around (under one name or other) since 1920 and the Packers since 1921.

What may surprise you is that there has been at least one Hall of Famer on fifty-three different team rosters. Of course, many of those teams no longer exist. Of the current National Football League teams, only the Atlanta Falcons, Cincinnati Bengals, New England Patriots, Seattle Seahawks, and Tampa Bay Buccaneers have yet to have a former player, coach, or executive enshrined. This undoubtedly will change, however, as more and more individuals become eligible for election to the Hall of Fame.

Is it true that an NFL franchise once sold for $1?

As hard as this is to believe, it's true. It happened in 1926 when Ole Haugsrud and Dewey Scanlon purchased the Duluth Kelleys for $1. But for their dollar, they got not only a pretty lousy team, but also its debts, which were large.

Haugsrud's plan was to sign his long-time friend and Stanford All-America running back Ernie Nevers to a pro contract as a player-coach.

Nevers was the best-known athlete coming out of college and Haugsrud felt that his gate appeal would assure the team's success. Unfortunately, the rival American Football League offered Nevers a very big contract. Out of friendship for Haugsrud, Nevers agreed to play for Duluth if Haugsrud would match the AFL's offer of $15,000 and 25 percent of the gate. Haugsrud agreed. He even changed the team name to Ernie Nevers's Eskimos.

Haugsrud was determined to make the Eskimos a success. Even his players tried to help. Realizing that by having Nevers on their team, they would be able to schedule more games, they agreed to play for only $50 a game if they lost, $60 if they tied, and $75 if they won.

As a part of his plan, Haugsrud made the Eskimos a traveling team. After two games at home, the Eskimos set out on a coast-to-coast journey that included more than twenty games. To keep expenses down, the Eskimos rarely traveled with more than fifteen players. Can you imagine playing sixty minutes of football with just fifteen players? The famous sportswriter Grantland Rice was so impressed that he named them "the Iron Men of the North."

Just as Haugsrud had predicted, Nevers was a tremendous gate attraction. He was also a tremendous player. He did most of the ball-carrying and passing and all of the placekicking and punting. He even returned kickoffs and punts and played defense. In fact, during the entire season, Nevers missed only twenty-six minutes of playing time, when doctors ordered him to sit out a game in Milwaukee. But when his team fell behind, he put himself back in the game and threw a touchdown pass to defeat Milwaukee, 7–6.

In 1926, the Eskimos were a financial success. However, the 1927 season was much less successful and in 1928 the team didn't operate at all. Finally, Haugsrud, encouraged by the league, agreed to sell his team. When he did, the league promised that if ever another team was granted in the state of Minnesota, Haugsrud would be given an opportunity to purchase it. In 1960, when it was announced that the Minnesota Vikings would join the NFL the next year, Haugsrud reminded the league of its promise and purchased 10 percent of the team. Not bad, considering it all started with a $1 investment.

As for Ernie Nevers, he went on to become player-coach of the Chicago Cardinals from 1929 to 1931. He later pitched for the St. Louis Browns and played professional basketball. Even though his NFL career was brief—five years—he was elected to the Pro Football Hall of Fame.

Ole Haugsrud's $1 investment in the Eskimos paid off with the Vikings.

What's the difference between the National Football Conference and the American Football Conference?

The National Football League is made up of two fourteen-team conferences. One is the American Football Conference (AFC) and the other is the National Football Conference (NFC). Each conference has three divisions: the Eastern, Central, and Western. The only difference between the two conferences is the teams that play in them.

The NFL's present two-conference structure began in 1970. It was the final result of the merger between the NFL and the American Football League. Beginning that year, the AFL was to become the American Football Conference and the NFL the National Football Conference.

However, before that could happen, a problem had to be resolved. Since the NFL had sixteen teams and the AFL had only ten, three teams from the NFL had to shift to the AFC so there would be equal-sized conferences. Deciding which teams would shift was not an easy matter. The AFL and NFL had been bitterly at war with each other for several years before the merger. There was still some rancor between the two leagues. Also, some NFL owners worried about how their fans might react to their teams playing AFC teams instead of the NFL rivals they were used to.

Finally, during a meeting of NFL owners, Art Rooney, owner of the Pittsburgh Steelers, broke the deadlock. "I'll go," he announced. Within seconds, Art Modell of the Cleveland Browns declared, "If Rooney goes, I go too." Next, Baltimore Colts owner Carroll Rosenbloom added, "Make it three." The merger was complete and the NFL had its conferences.

In 1976, each conference grew by one team when the Tampa Bay Buccaneers and the Seattle Seahawks joined the NFL. Today, the conferences look like this:

American Football Conference

Buffalo Bills
Cincinnati Bengals
Cleveland Browns
Denver Broncos
Houston Oilers
Indianapolis Colts
Kansas City Chiefs
Los Angeles Raiders
Miami Dolphins
New England Patriots
New York Jets
Pittsburgh Steelers
San Diego Chargers
Seattle Seahawks

National Football Conference

Atlanta Falcons
Chicago Bears
Dallas Cowboys
Detroit Lions
Green Bay Packers
Los Angeles Rams
Minnesota Vikings
New Orleans Saints
New York Giants
Philadelphia Eagles
Phoenix Cardinals
San Francisco 49ers
Tampa Bay Buccaneers
Washington Redskins

Who was the greatest running back of all time?

Oh boy, that's a tough question. There are so many to consider. In pro football's early years there were outstanding runners, such as Jim Thorpe and Ernie Nevers. Unfortunately, since pro football kept no official records until 1933, most of what we know about players from that period comes from sometimes less-than-reliable newspaper accounts or stories passed down through the years. In any case, we do know that both men were more than just running backs. They were also great kickers, accomplished passers, and played defense as well. So to attempt to compare them—or other runners who were two-way players, like Bronko Nagurski or Red Grange—with

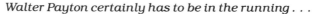

Walter Payton certainly has to be in the running . . .

running backs from later years is really unfair.

In the years following World War II, there were several great running backs in the NFL. In 1944, rookie running back Steve Van Buren of the Philadelphia Eagles led the National Football League in punt returns. The next year he led the league in rushing (something he would do three more times), scoring, and kickoff returns. In 1947, he became only the second running back to gain more than 1,000 yards rushing in a season.

Another great running back of that era was Marion Motley of the Cleveland Browns. Though he never had a 1,000-yard season, he was one of the most powerful runners of all time. He averaged almost 6 yards every time he carried the ball and as a blocker he could knock just about anyone flat.

Many NFL fans from the 1950s and 1960s claim that halfback Hugh McElhenny was the most exciting runner of all time. The King, as he was nicknamed, would run from sideline to sideline before breaking away for a long gain, leaving confused defenders in his dust. Chicago Bears great Gale Sayers was another exciting runner. Opponents knew that any time Sayers had the ball it was a potential touchdown. Sayers probably had the quickest acceleration of any running back in his era.

In 1973, O. J. Simpson became the first running back to rush for more than 2,000 yards in a season. Add to that the fact that he gained over 1,000 yards five seasons in a row and you have a pretty good argument for considering the Juice the greatest runner.

However, in my opinion, "the greatest" comes down to a decision between Jim Brown of the Cleveland Browns and Walter Payton of the Chicago Bears.

Jim Brown was to many the perfect running back. He had speed and

. . . and so does Jim Brown.

strength. During his brilliant career, which lasted from 1957 to 1965, Brown shattered virtually every rushing record in the book. He led the league in rushing eight times, was an All-NFL pick eight times, and played in the Pro Bowl nine times. When he retired he held twenty NFL records, including an unbelievable career rushing record of 12,312 yards.

Brown shocked the pro football world in the summer of 1966 with the announcement that he was retiring. Most felt that he was at the peak of his career. In fact, just a few months earlier he was awarded the Jim Thorpe Trophy as the NFL's Most Valuable Player.

On the other hand, when Walter Payton of the Chicago Bears retired in 1987, he had completed a full thirteen-season career, during which he missed just one game. During his career, he rushed for more than 1,000 yards eight times. In a game against the Minnesota Vikings in 1977, Payton set a single-game rushing record of 275 yards.

Payton wasn't as fast as Jim Brown, but he had just as much strength and was more versatile. Not only was he a reliable receiver out of the backfield, but on occasion he also passed the ball on the option play and he was a devastating blocker. "He'll run with it, catch it, and block for you. He's the very best," Bears head coach Mike Ditka once remarked. When asked about his blocking, Payton once said, "I love it. This is what the game is made of. Anybody can run the ball. But to be able to run, catch, and block . . . is totally awesome."

So who gets my vote for the "greatest running back?" Well, I know this won't please everyone, but I give a slight edge to the "totally awesome" Walter Payton.

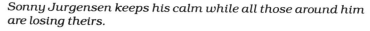

What is the most difficult position to play?

Without a doubt, quarterback is the most difficult position to play. A quarterback has to be able to do so many things well. He must be able to pass the ball long distances accurately, run the ball when necessary, and read defenses correctly to determine play selection.

Also, a quarterback must be strong

Sonny Jurgensen keeps his calm while all those around him are losing theirs.

and courageous. Remember, defensive players are out to "sack" the quarterback. Speed and quick thinking are important. A quarterback must make decisions without hesitation. This requires him to be confident in his abilities. A quarterback's confidence is often contagious among his teammates. Above all, the quarterback must be a leader.

That's not to say that a quarterback can win games all by himself. Of course not. He needs his linemen to block. He needs receivers to run perfect patterns and catch his passes. He needs power and speed from his running backs. And he needs a good defense to keep the opponent from scoring more points.

However, there is no more important player on the field than the quarterback. He is the man who controls the offense, the guy who has to get the job done. The quarterback is the field general.

Who was the best quarterback in pro football history?

Pro football has produced many great quarterbacks.

Sammy Baugh, who played for the Washington Redskins from 1937 to 1952, was the game's first highly publicized passer. Slinging Sammy, as he was known, did much to make the forward pass a major offensive weapon in pro football.

Another great quarterback was Bobby Layne. Layne, who played from the late 1940s to the early 1960s, mostly with the Detroit Lions and Pittsburgh Steelers, wasn't known as a great passer but was one of the finest field generals the game ever produced. He was a gutsy player who never gave up. One of Layne's teammates once remarked, "Bobby never lost a game. Sometimes time just ran out on him."

Dallas Cowboys great Roger Staubach could pass and run with equal ease. He also had a remarkable ability to rally his team to come-from-behind wins. In fact, he led the Cowboys to twenty-three fourth-quarter comeback victories.

There are other great quarterbacks that deserve consideration. Players such as Terry Bradshaw of the Pitts-

Was it the Colts' Johnny Unitas?

68

Or the Browns' Otto Graham?

Otto takes flight while others fight.

burgh Steelers, Fran Tarkenton of the Minnesota Vikings, Sonny Jurgensen of the Eagles and the Redskins, and Dan Fouts of the San Diego Chargers, just to mention a few.

But when it gets right down to "the best," it all comes down to a choice between Johnny Unitas of the Baltimore Colts and Otto Graham of the Cleveland Browns.

The Johnny Unitas story is a rags-to-riches tale of determination. A ninth-round draft choice of the Pittsburgh Steelers in 1955, Unitas was cut before he even threw one pass in a preseason game. Disappointed but not defeated, the Pittsburgh native kept his hopes alive by playing semipro football for $6 a week with a local team. After the season ended, a fan wrote to Baltimore Colts coach Weeb Ewbank, telling him of Unitas and suggesting that he was "an outstanding prospect."

Ewbank decided to give Unitas a chance. He signed him to a $7,000 contract on a make-it basis. That was all the chance Johnny U. needed. After the Colts' regular quarterback George Shaw went down with injuries in the fourth game of the 1956 season, Unitas became the Colts' starting quarterback. He held the job for the next seventeen seasons and was voted into the Pro Football Hall of Fame when his career was over.

During his career, Unitas passed over 40,000 yards and 290 touchdowns. He was All-NFL five times, three-time NFL Player of the Year, and appeared in ten Pro Bowls.

Though he gave many brilliant performances, without a doubt his most famous was in the 1958 NFL Championship Game against the New York Giants. Before a national television audience, Unitas displayed all the characteristics of a truly great quarterback. Under tremendous pressure, he demonstrated his passing and leadership skills while calling all the right plays at the right time. Trailing the Giants, 17–14, with just over two minutes to play, Unitas engineered a drive that led to a field goal that sent the game into overtime. In overtime, Unitas engineered a brilliant 80-yard drive to win, 23–17.

In 1946, when Paul Brown began organizing the Cleveland Browns to play in the new All-America Football Conference, he chose Otto Graham to be his quarterback. And with Graham at the controls, the Browns became a pro football power.

If a team's success is a measure of its leader's greatness, then Otto Graham must surely have been the best. During his ten-year career with the Browns, Graham led his team to ten divisional or league championships. He was All-Pro nine times and was the leading passer for four years in the AAFC and for two years in the NFL.

Even though Graham led the Browns to four consecutive AAFC titles, 1946 through 1949, there were some who minimized his accomplishments by claiming that the AAFC was inferior to the older NFL. However, in 1950, after the Browns joined the NFL, Graham quickly made believers of pro football fans everywhere. After coasting to a 10–2 record in the regular season, Graham led the Browns to a 30–28 victory over the Los Angeles Rams in the NFL Championship Game. Although the game was played on a frozen Cleveland Stadium field amid snow flurries, Graham passed for four touchdowns and nearly 300 yards.

Graham's greatest single-game performance, however, came in the 1953 NFL Championship Game against the Detroit Lions. In that game, not only did Graham pass for three touchdowns but he ran for three more, destroying the Lions, 56–10.

Who was the best quarterback? Well, I tend to favor the man who took his team to the playoffs every year.

What was the largest crowd ever to attend a pro football game?

The largest crowd ever to attend a pro football game was 105,840. It wasn't a Super Bowl or a title game that attracted such a huge crowd. For that matter, it wasn't even a regular season game. It was the 1947 College All-Star Game between the Chicago Bears and a team of College All-Stars.

The game was an annual event that matched the NFL champion against the College All-Stars. It began in 1934 as the brainchild of Arch Ward, sports editor of the *Chicago Tribune*. Originally designed to be a onetime event, it became the longest continuing series played exclusively for charity in pro football's history. During the forty-two years that the game was played, ending in 1976, the College All-Star Game raised more than $13 million for the *Chicago Tribune* charities.

In additon to raising money for charity, the game also gave pro football a chance to showcase itself and prove it was at least as good as the college version of the game back when college football was king. However, the 1947 game, in which the all-time attendance record was set, did little to promote the quality of NFL play. The College All-Stars shut out the Bears, 16–0.

How did quarterbacks, halfbacks, and fullbacks get their names?

In today's version of football, a fullback is usually positioned next to his halfback running mate. However, in football's early days, a fullback was positioned behind the halfback. He was said to be "all the way" or "the full way" back. A halfback, as the name implies, was "halfway" back between the fullback and line of scrimmage. Following the same pattern, a quarterback lined up "a quarter of the way" back between the fullback and line of scrimmage. Confusing? Well, just think of the names as a description of where the players were originally positioned.

What is the difference between offside and encroachment?

While the difference between encroachment and offside would be easy to demonstrate, it's not as easy to explain. The best way to start is to explain two other terms: "line of scrimmage" and "neutral zone."

According to the *NFL Professional Football Rules*: The line of scrimmage for each team is a yard line passing through the end of the ball nearest a team's own goal line." Put another way, each side—offense and defense—has its own line of scrimmage. The defensive line of scrimmage starts behind the end of the ball closest to their own goal line. The offensive line of scrimmage starts behind the other point of the ball.

Now, the area between the two lines of scrimmage, which is equal to the length of the football, is called the neutral zone.

A player is encroaching when any part of his body is in the neutral zone and *contact with an opposing player* is made before the snap of the ball. A player is offside when any part of his body *crosses his scrimmage line* before the ball is snapped. The center is allowed in the neutral zone as long as he is not beyond the defense's scrimmage line because he must be over the ball in order to snap it back.

Both encroachment and offside are 5-yard penalties.

Something to keep in mind is that a

player is not offside if he gets back on-side before the ball is snapped. On the other hand, if he makes any contact with the opponent, he is encroaching. When encroaching occurs, the official immediately blows his whistle and stops play. The point of both rules is to prevent either team from entering the neutral zone first.

Have the Detroit Lions
always played on Thanksgiving Day?

Turkey, dressing, potatoes, gravy, and the Detroit Lions, that's a Thanksgiving Day menu for millions of football fans every year. I know it has been in my house for as long as I can remember.

The tradition of the Lions playing on Thanksgiving Day began in 1934. That's when G. A. Richards brought the Lions to Detroit from Portsmouth, Ohio, where the team was known as the Spartans. Richards, the owner of a Detroit radio station, felt a Thanksgiving Day game would be an excellent way to promote his new team. This wasn't a new idea. For many years high schools and colleges had played on Thanksgiving Day. It was just a new concept for the pros.

Knowing the value of radio,

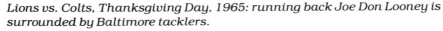

Lions vs. Colts, Thanksgiving Day, 1965: running back Joe Don Looney is surrounded by Baltimore tacklers.

Richards, along with NBC Radio, set up a 94-station network to broadcast the Turkey Day game. The response was immediate. The game was a national hit, and except for a six-year period from 1939 through 1944 when the series was temporarily discontinued, the Lions have played on every Thanksgiving Day. The holiday special helped make the Lions one of the better known NFL teams across the country.

For the first five years of the Turkey Day game, the Chicago Bears were the Lions' opponents. After the six-year pause with no Thanksgiving Day play, the Lions played and lost to five different teams. However, the losing skid ended in 1950 with a lopsided 49–14 victory over the New York Yanks.

In 1951, the Lions played the Green Bay Packers in the first of what would become an extremely popular 13-game annual rivalry. The Lions dominated the series, winning nine, losing three and tying one. Due principally to the Packers complaining about having to play the midweek game, the format was changed in 1964 to bring a different opponent each year to the Lions' den.

Though there have been several memorable Thanksgiving Day games, one I will never forget is the 1976 game between the Lions and Buffalo Bills. Even though the Lions beat the Bills 27–14, Buffalo running back O. J. Simpson stole the show. Simpson, running against a Lions' defense which at the time was the best in the NFL, rushed for a then-NFL-record 273 yards. Though it may have been just another Thanksgiving Day win for the Lions, for Simpson, it was one step closer to being elected to the Hall of Fame.

I know that football card collecting is becoming a popular hobby. What can you tell me about the hobby?

According to James Beckett, a leading authority on sports cards and author of several books on the subject, football cards are relatively new on the scene. Although there was a college football set produced in 1890 by Mayo Cut Plug, a chewing tobacco company, it wasn't until 1935, when the National Chicle Company issued a 36-card set, that football cards were again produced. There was, however, a multisport set issued in 1933 by Goudey Sport Kings, which included three football stars—Red Grange, Jim Thorpe, and Knute Rockne.

Unlike baseball cards, however, football cards disappeared from candy store shelves from 1935 until 1948. In that year both the Bowman and Leaf chewing gum companies issued football card sets. Since then, football card sets of one kind or another have been issued annually.

During the early 1950s, the Bowman company was virtually unchallenged in the football card business. However, in 1956, Topps, which had produced sets in 1950, 1951, and 1955, purchased the Bowman company. Since then, Topps has produced a major football card set every year.

There have been several other companies that have produced football cards, such as Fleer, Bazooka, Coca-

Cola, Kahn's, McDonald's, Post Cereal, Bell Brand, and Score. However, in 1989, the National Football League became the first major league sport ever to issue an official card set, the NFL Pro set.

Though it has not yet matched the popularity of baseball cards, the interest in football cards as collectibles has grown tremendously during the last few years. Beckett cites two principal reasons for the increase: the fantastic growth of the sports memorabilia collecting hobby, and the "continuing and increasing popularity of the sport itself."

This increased interest in football cards means an increased value to collectors. Like baseball cards, football cards are collected by some for investment. There are several periodicals available today that deal specifically with the value of sports cards as investments. Each year there are hundreds of card shows where dealers and collectors alike buy, sell, and trade sports cards. As more and more collectors and dealers discover football cards, their value increases as a result of limited supply.

If collecting football cards interests you, you might want to pick up a copy of Beckett's *The Sport Americana Football, Hockey, Basketball, and Boxing Card Price Guide*. Also, a subscription to any one of several periodicals on the subject, such as *Sports Collector's Digest* or *Football Card News*, would be very helpful and enjoyable for the novice or the experienced collector.

What was the longest run from scrimmage ever?

Well, you can't run any farther than Tony Dorsett did on January 3, 1983, against the Minnesota Vikings. The Dallas Cowboys' great running back electrified a "Monday Night Football" television audience when he dashed 99 yards—the longest distance a player can run from scrimmage—for a touchdown.

Dorsett's run, though an NFL record, was actually a broken play. Dorsett wasn't even the intended ball carrier. The ball carrier was supposed to be fullback Ron Springs. However, Springs thought the formation was "Jay Hawk," which called for him to leave the field. When Cowboys quarterback Danny White turned to hand the ball to his fullback, Springs was on the sidelines watching, and the Cowboys had only ten men on the field.

Without hesitating, Dorsett took charge. "I was just thinking of getting out of the backfield," he stated. Realizing the situation, he took the hand-off from White, burst through the Vikings' line, and, using his sprinter's speed, dashed down the right sideline for a 99-yard touchdown.

For the game, Dorsett carried the ball 16 times for 153 yards. Unfortunately, even after such a fine performance, the Cowboys were unable to hold their slim 27–24 fourth quarter lead. With just 1 minute and 52 seconds remaining to be played, Vikings quarterback Tommy Kramer passed 14 yards to Rickey Young for a touchdown and a 31–27 Vikings victory.

Has anyone ever blocked more than one kick in the same game?

While I'm sure the answer is yes, there is no official record that lists blocked kicks. However, I once read an old newspaper account of how, in 1941, Philadelphia Eagles guard Bob Suffridge not only blocked three kicks in a single game, but on the same play. That's right, the same kick—three times.

Here's how it happened. After the Washington Redskins pulled ahead of the Eagles, 20–14, late in the fourth quarter in a very close game, Suffridge reasoned the Eagles still had a chance to win if he blocked the extra point. As the center snapped the ball, Suffridge burst through the line and blocked it. However, there was a penalty on the play. The official ruled that another Eagle lineman had jumped offside. So Suffridge had to do it all over again. And he did.

This time, however, after Suffridge blocked the kick, the ball bounced out-

Bob Suffridge accomplished one of the strangest feats in NFL history.

of-bounds. The rules of the day were such that a ball blocked out of bounds before being recovered meant the offense, in this case the Redskins, would get yet another chance to kick the extra point. But Suffridge was determined. Again the two-time all-America star burst through the Redskins' line. This time he took no chances. Not only did he block the kick for a third time, but

he wrapped it in his arms and lay on top of it until the official blew it dead.

Unfortunately, the Eagles weren't able to capitalize on Suffridge's outstanding play. They were unable to add any additional points, so the Redskins held on to win, 20–14. However, though he was just a rookie, Suffridge was named to the league's All-Star team that year.

Who invented the huddle?

While nobody is absolutely certain who invented the huddle, the most widely accepted theory is that it was first used by players at Gallaudet College in Washington, D.C., back in 1894. Gallaudet College is a school devoted to deaf students. The huddle was supposedly developed there as a matter of necessity. You see, the sign language used by deaf students is a visual language. It can be seen and understood at a considerable distance, much farther than words spoken in a hushed tone can be heard. So when the Gallaudet varsity team practiced against their second team, they had to conceal their hand signals which could be easily read by the underclassmen. And so the huddle was born.

The huddle was such a logical way for teams to group together and discuss their strategy that in no time it was accepted as a traditional part of the game. However, over the years even the huddle has come under attack. For instance, in 1945 the Washington Redskins attempted to discard the huddle and simply call their plays at the line of scrimmage. While this strategy didn't work, it was a predecessor of the "hurry-up" or "no-huddle" offenses

commonly used today in the last few minutes of a half.

More recently, the Cincinnati Bengals successfully used a no-huddle offense. Some opposing coaches, however, were irked by the Bengals' format. The Cincinnati version of the no-huddle was designed to run off a series of plays and confuse defenses. Some coaches felt that what the Bengals were really trying to do was draw a penalty. The Bengals were accused of putting more than eleven offensive players on the field, then running some of them off quickly. While opponents scambled to make sure they had the right defense on the field, the Bengals called for a quick snap and often caught the opposition offside.

An official statement by the NFL before the January 8, 1989 American Football Conference Championship Game between the Bengals and the Buffalo Bills banned any quick snap aimed at drawing a penalty on the defense. Though the Bengals still won 21–10, the ruling angered Cincinnati coach Sam Wyche.

During the off-season, league officials and coaches met and discussed the Bengals' no-huddle or quick-snap offense. It was decided that the offense was not "illegal or unethical." According to the Bengals, all they were doing was running a two-minute drill throughout the game. Who would have ever imagined such controversy over the huddle?

I've heard of a play called the "Alley Oop." What is it?

The "Alley Oop" was a pass developed by the San Francisco 49ers in 1957. Actually, it was a busted play between the Hall of Fame quarterback Y. A. Tittle and rookie receiver R. C. Owens. The play was born during a practice

R. C. Owens, master of the Alley Oop.

session when Tittle prepared to pass to Owens. Tittle, however, had to delay his throw because Owens had run too far downfield. When he finally released his pass, an onrushing lineman hit his arm, causing the ball to arc high in the air. Owens, realizing his mistake, quickly circled back. Unfortunately, so did three defensive backs. However, Owens, who stood 6′ 3″, outleaped all three and made the reception. Impressed by Owens's leaping ability, the 49ers' coaches added the play to their playbooks.

Together Tittle and Owens refined the rather unusual play. Owens per-fected his leaping and Tittle was al-most perfect at getting the ball to him. Owens actually asked Tittle not to throw a spiral, but rather to make the ball "wobble a little" so he could better judge the timing of his leap.

The "Alley Oop" enabled the 49ers to win three games in the final seconds and tie for the Western Conference title with the Detroit Lions. However, the unusual play wasn't enough to defeat the Lions in the Conference playoff game. Although Tittle ignited the 49ers' offense with a 27–7 halftime lead, the Lions roared back in the sec-ond half to win 31–27.

Is it true that an NFL team once drafted the same player twice?

Yes, it is true. In 1946, the Washington Redskins chose UCLA halfback Cal Rossi as their first-round draft selec-tion. However, there was one small problem with the selection: Rossi was just a junior and wasn't eligible for the draft. The next year, as if once were not enough, the Redskins again selected Rossi as their number one pick. This time, though he was eligible, Rossi simply chose not to play pro football.

Why is the Hall of Fame located in Canton, Ohio?

Historical ties to the game and a well-organized civic campaign is what brought the Hall of Fame to Canton, Ohio. The idea was first placed before the public on December 6, 1959, when the Canton Repository headlined a challenge that read, "PRO FOOTBALL NEEDS A HALL OF FAME AND LOGI-CAL SITE IS HERE."

Why was Canton a logical site? Well, actually there were three very good his-torical reasons. First, though it was originally known as the American Pro-fessional Football Association, the NFL was organized in Canton in 1920. Sec-ondly, Canton was for many years the home of the Canton Bulldogs, an early-day pro football power, even before the days of the NFL. The Bulldogs were also a charter member of the NFL and the league's first two-time champion. A third historical tie to the game was

Where the NFL was born in 1920: the Hupmobile auto showroom in the Odd Fellows' Building in Canton, Ohio.

that Jim Thorpe, pro football's first big-name player and the NFL's first president, played for the Bulldogs from 1915 to 1920.

Armed with those historical facts and the commitment of civic leaders, a formal bid to the NFL was made on January 25, 1961, for acceptance of Canton as the site for a pro football Hall of Fame. Three months later Canton was approved and a building fund drive began. By February 8, 1962, the civic fund-raising campaign acquired pledges of $378,026, and on August 11, 1962, ground was broken.

The Hall opened on September 7, 1963, as a two-building complex. There have been two expansions since, and the Hall is now a four-building 51,000-square-foot facility.

The Hall truly has something for everyone. Besides serving as an honoring spot for the game's greatest stars, it also represents the sport in many other colorful and entertaining ways. In-cluded are four large exhibition areas where the history of pro football from 1892 to the present is detailed in memento, picture, and story form. There's also a 350-seat theater that shows a different NFL film every hour, and a complete research library. And, of course, if you're like me you can't visit a museum or attraction without stopping by the souvenir shop, and, boy, does the Hall of Fame have a great one.

The Hall is open every day except Christmas. If you'd like more information about the Hall, all you have to do is write to the Pro Football Hall of Fame, 2121 George Halas Drive N.W., Canton, OH 44708.

Has the NFL always had the twenty-eight teams it has now?

The National Football League has only had its current twenty-eight-team membership since 1976. That's when the Tampa Bay Buccaneers and the Seattle Seahawks were added as expansion teams. But that was hardly the first time that the league's size and member teams had changed. While the NFL has never had more teams than its current twenty-eight, it has had as few as eight teams (in 1932).

In the NFL's early years, teams were located mostly in small cities or towns. There were teams in places like Canton, Columbus, and Dayton, Ohio; Muncie, Indiana; Rochester, New York; and Racine, Wisconsin. Obviously, none of these teams are still members of the NFL. However, you'll probably be surprised to learn that two original members of the NFL, the Decatur Staleys and the Chicago Cardinals, still exist. The Staleys are the Chicago Bears and the Chicago Cardinals are the Phoenix Cardinals.

Like the Cardinals and Bears, several other active NFL teams began in other cities. In the American Football Conference, the Indianapolis Colts began as the Baltimore Colts, the Kansas City Chiefs were originally the Dallas Texans, the Los Angeles Raiders were in Oakland, and the San Diego Chargers originally played in Los Angeles. In the National Football Conference, the Detroit Lions began as the Spartans of Portsmouth, Ohio, the Los Angeles Rams were originally from Cleveland, and the Washington Redskins were the Boston Braves.

Are there any unbreakable records in pro football?

When Cleveland Browns running back Jim Brown retired in 1965, people thought no one would ever break his career rushing record of 12,312 yards. But then along came Walter Payton. By the time Payton ended his thirteen-year career with the Chicago Bears, he had amassed 16,726 yards rushing.

However, there is a pro football record that was set even before Brown's retirement that I think just might be unbreakable. It belongs to former Bal-timore Colts superstar quarterback Johnny Unitas.

From 1956 to 1960, Unitas had a re-markable string of 47 straight games in which he threw at least one touch-down pass. Comparing it to the next-best mark, a 30-game TD-passing string by Dan Marino of the Miami Dol-phins, illustrates just how extraordi-nary Unitas's record is.

Unitas' exceptional feat began in the ninth game of his rookie season—

Johnny Unitas (left) and Ray Berry (right) flank coach Weeb Ewbank, who runs the film projector as the Colts prepare for the 1958 title game. The Colts, who had already clinched a spot in the contest, were still uncertain whether their opponents would be the Browns or the Giants.

against the Los Angeles Rams. Coincidentally, the streak also ended against the Rams, eleven games into the 1960 season.

In the 47-game string Unitas completed 697 passes for 10,645 yards and 102 touchdowns. Seven times he threw four touchdown passes in a game, and nine times he threw three. Although the 697 passes were spread out among seven different receivers, Raymond Berry with 38 TD receptions and Lenny Moore with 27 were definitely Johnny's favorite targets. All three, by the way, are enshrined in the Pro Football Hall of Fame.

If you'd like to know more about the Baltimore Colts or Johnny Unitas, you might get a copy of *The Baltimore Colts* or of *The Greatest Football Game Ever Played*, both by John Steadman.

Why is the game called football?

Like the game itself, the word "football" has foreign ancestors. Historians trace American football back to two European cousins, soccer and rugby. Both began as kicking games.

Soccer—the most popular sport in the world—was originally known as "association football." Newspapers seeking a shorter phrase began to refer to it as "assoc." That name was soon shortened to "soc" and then grew back a bit, to "soccer."

While rugby also began as a *foot*ball game, in 1823 something occurred that changed the kicking game forever. A player named William Webb Ellis, instead of kicking the ball over the goal line, picked it up and ran it across. At first, observers didn't know what to think. Eventually, they agreed it was a good idea. The game was played at the Rugby School and became known as rugby football, later shortened to rugby.

Both soccer-style football and rugby-style football eventually found their way to America. What resulted was an American combination of the two games. It wasn't until much later (1906) that forward passing was allowed. So because the American game was really just another form of the European football games, it too became known as football.

What are some of the more unusual items in the Hall of Fame?

The Hall of Fame has hundreds of great mementos of pro football's past and present, including some rather unusual ones. Just to mention a few, there are a pair of ice tongs; a trophy made from coal; a contract that calls for a pay cut if the game is played at night; a quarterback's wristband with the plays written on it; and a helmet equipped with a radio receiver.

The multilevel displays and spiraling ramps of the Hall of Fame in Canton provide an unusual and exciting setting for a tribute to pro football's history and heroes.

The ice tongs belonged to Hall of Fame halfback Red Grange, who was the biggest name in college and pro football during the 1920s. While playing for the University of Illinois, Grange earned the nickname of "the Galloping Ghost" after an October 18, 1924, performance in which he ran for four touchdowns in the first twelve minutes. Red also earned another nickname reflective of his off-the-field work: because he worked as an ice delivery man during his college summers in Wheaton, Illinois, Red became known as "the Wheaton Iceman." Grange once explained that he kept the physically demanding job because lifting and carrying the huge blocks of ice was a great way to stay in shape.

Another unusual item found on display at the Hall is a football-shaped trophy that was made from a single, highly polished piece of coal. The glistening black prize was presented to the members of the 1925 Pottsville Maroons by their fans. It seems the Pottsville fans, many of whom were coal miners, felt their team was unjustly denied the 1925 NFL championship crown. The facts disagree. Actually, the Maroons were expelled from the league after they played an exhibition game in

Yes, it's all made from coal, like the coal that's placed in the stockings of undeserving children at Christmas. But you've got to give the Pottsville rooters credit for having their hearts in the right place.

the protected territory of another league team, the Frankford Yellow Jackets. This was a clear and very serious rules violation. With the Maroons out of the league, the Chicago Cardinals went on to finish the season with the best record and were awarded the 1925 NFL crown. However, Pottsville fans insisted they were robbed. So using coal, the natural resource so important to their community, the Maroons' faithful presented the team with their own version of a championship trophy. Inscribed on the coal football are the words, "Pottsville Maroons NFL and World Champions 1925."

Another team from the NFL's early years was the Providence Steam Roller. Though they were members of the NFL for just seven seasons, 1925–31, the Steam Roller's management was responsible for at least one NFL "first" and a unique memento for the Hall of Fame. On November 3, 1929, the Steam Roller became the first NFL team to host a game at night under floodlights. Due to the game's success, the lights were permanently installed the following season.

While floodlights may not have had an immediate effect on the game of pro football, they did have an immediate effect on at least one Steam Roller player. According to his 1930 contract, which is now in the Hall of Fame files, Tony Latone was paid $125 "for all league daylight games and sixty percent of that sum for all league floodlight games." Former team executive Pearce Johnson once explained that the reduction in pay for floodlight games was arranged by the team's general manager to help pay the installation costs of the floodlights. It is not likely that players today would agree to such a scheme.

"Unusual" is really the only word to adequately describe Tom Matte's wristband and the story behind the final games of the Baltimore Colts' 1965 season. First, with just three games remaining, the Colts lost the services of their starting quarterback, Johnny Unitas, who was out with a knee injury. A week later, against the Green Bay Packers, backup quarterback Gary Cuozzo was sidelined with a shoulder injury. Halfback Tom Matte was forced into duty as Cuozzo's emergency replacement. At first, Cuozzo's injury didn't appear to be too serious and he returned to finish the game. Unfortunately, his return wasn't enough; the Colts lost.

After the game it was learned that Cuozzo's injury was more serious than first thought. Reluctantly, coach Don Shula notified Matte that he was to be the starting quarterback for the Colts' final game, which was against the Los Angeles Rams. Adding to the pressure of having to play quarterback, Matte knew that in order to keep their playoff hopes alive the Colts had to defeat or tie the Rams.

Immediately, Matte began a quarter-

The Canton Bulldogs were a legendary pro football team in the years before the coming of the National Football League. Hall of Famer Jim Thorpe was their most famous player.

backing cram course. He studied films, met with coaches, and practiced passing drills. Though he studied diligently, Matte feared it wasn't enough. He decided the solution might be to write the offensive plays on a small piece of paper and attach it to his wristband. "It was helpful," he remarked after the Rams game, "because sometimes in the huddle your mind goes blank." In fact, some of his teammates later recalled how Matte called his first play in the huddle. "Out right, flank left," he shouted nervously. "I mean, out left, flank right," he corrected, causing some linemen to laugh. Finally, after referring to his wristband, the reluctant quarterback shouted confidently, "Out left, wing right." From then on it was smooth sailing. The Colts pulled off a stunning upset. They defeated the Rams 21–17. Thanks in part to his wristband, which is now on display at the Hall, Matte was an instant celebrity. Unfortunately, the following week the Colts were defeated 13–10 in overtime by the Green Bay Packers in a playoff game for first place in the Western Conference.

Perhaps the most unusual item in the Hall's collection, however, is a football helmet designed in 1956 by two Ohio inventors, John Campbell and George Sarles. What they developed was something called a "Radio Helmet System." It was first thought of by Sarles, who noticed the delays in Cleveland Browns football games caused by coach Paul Brown's system of sending in play calls with substitute players. Sarles approached Brown with the idea of developing a system that would allow him to talk directly to his quarterback in the huddle. He proposed putting a radio receiver in quarterback George Ratterman's helmet. Brown liked the idea, but insisted that its development be kept a secret.

Next Sarles enlisted the help of

From 1938 through 1946, the Most Valuable Player in the National Football League was awarded this impressive trophy, named for Joe Carr, the league's president from 1921 until his death in 1939.

The 1930s were a fascinating time in pro football, filled with rules innovations, great stars, and classic contests. Offenses opened up, and for the first time passes filled the air. Two-platoon football was still in the distance. Most players played the entire game on both offense and defense. They had to be strong and skilled.

Campbell. Together the two developed a miniaturized receiver that could pick up voice messages sent from a transmitter. The radio receiver was carefully inserted into a Browns helmet for testing.

Once, while they were testing how far away the receiver could pick up a signal, their secret was almost exposed. Wearing the helmet, Sarles walked into a wooded area behind Campbell's home. Sarles was supposed to return when the signals from Campbell became too weak to hear. After sev-

eral minutes, Campbell became concerned that something had happened to his partner. So he stopped the transmission and drove around the block about a quarter of a mile behind his house. There he spotted Sarles still wearing the helmet talking to a police officer. It turned out the police officer had picked up their signals in his squad car. Thankfully, he was a Browns fan and agreed to keep his discovery confidential. Needless to say, the two inventors changed their frequency.

No, this is not a Halloween costume. Football players wore odd gear like this at the turn of the century. Moleskin pants, hip pads, and noseguards and earguards were the order of the day; yet to come were leather helmets and shoulder pads, not to mention hard helmets, faceguards, knee braces, and the yards of adhesive tape in which today's linemen wrap themselves. But the game back then was football, just as it is today, and the men who played it were the athletes. History and tradition connect the game of yesterday with that of today.

The All-American Football Conference (AAFC) of 1946–49 gave birth to the Cleveland Browns, Baltimore Colts, San Francisco 49ers, who entered the NFL in 1950 when the rival league disbanded. The AAFC's wide-open style came to be the dominant style of the NFL as well.

The helmet was first tested under game conditions in an exhibition game between the Browns and the Detroit Lions. Coach Brown had the two inventors hide the transmitter behind a wooden light post. Throughout the first half, the system worked perfectly. Brown was able to communicate directly to his quarterback, George Ratterman. However, when the Lions' coaching staff noticed that Brown was not making his usual substitutions for play calling, they suspected something was up. After halftime, a Lions' assistant coach spotted the transmitter on the sideline. From that point on, Ratterman was a marked man. Defensive linemen zeroed in on his helmet. At one point it was even torn from his head and punched. However, it continued to work perfectly.

News spread quickly and other teams began to develop their own helmet radio systems. None proved to be as effective as the Sarles-Campbell version. Unfortunately, after the Browns used the helmet in three more games, NFL Commissioner Bert Bell ruled that radio systems could not be used in NFL games. Forced into retirement, the helmet was all but forgotten until 1985, when John Campbell decided to donate the secret-weapon head gear to the Hall of Fame, where it took its place among pro football's other peculiar game mementos.

Pro football has seen plenty of great teams from the Canton Bulldogs of the 1910s up to the San Francisco 49ers of the late 1980s. The Steelers' Steel Curtain defense dominated the 1970s, but still left room for fans of the Miami Dolphins or Dallas Cowboys or Oakland Raiders to argue about who was really the best. In earlier years pro football's kings of the hill were the Green Bay Packers, or Cleveland Browns, or New York Giants, or Chicago Bears—you get the picture. Your favorite team's glory year may be next. That's one of the great things about this great game—every Sunday guarantees that something surprising, thrilling, even impossible, is bound to occur, and that if we only have faith, our heroes' turn (and ours) is sure to come.

First Games of Present NFL Teams

Team	Opponent	Date	Site
ATLANTA FALCONS	Los Angeles Rams	9/11/66	Atlanta
BUFFALO BILLS	New York Titans	9/11/60	New York
CHICAGO BEARS	Rock Island Independents	10/17/20	Rock Island
CINCINNATI BENGALS	San Diego Chargers	9/6/68	San Diego
CLEVELAND BROWNS	Miami Seahawks	9/6/46	Cleveland
DALLAS COWBOYS	Pittsburgh Steelers	9/24/60	Dallas
DENVER BRONCOS	Boston Patriots	9/9/60	Boston
DETROIT LIONS (Portsmouth Spartans)	Newark Tornadoes	9/14/30	Portsmouth
GREEN BAY PACKERS	Minneapolis Marines	10/23/21	Green Bay
HOUSTON OILERS	Oakland Raiders	9/11/60	San Francisco
INDIANAPOLIS COLTS (Baltimore Colts)	Chicago Bears	9/27/53	Baltimore
KANSAS CITY CHIEFS	Los Angeles Chargers	9/10/60	Los Angeles
LOS ANGELES RAIDERS (Oakland Raiders)	Houston Oilers	9/11/60	San Francisco
LOS ANGELES RAMS (Cleveland Rams)	Detroit Lions	9/10/37	Cleveland
MIAMI DOLPHINS	Oakland Raiders	9/2/66	Miami
MINNESOTA VIKINGS	Chicago Bears	9/17/61	Minneapolis
NEW ENGLAND PATRIOTS (Boston Patriots)	Denver Broncos	9/9/60	Boston
NEW ORLEANS SAINTS	Los Angeles Rams	9/17/67	Los Angeles
NEW YORK GIANTS	Providence Steamroller	10/11/25	Providence
NEW YORK JETS	Buffalo Bills	9/11/60	New York
PHILADELPHIA EAGLES	New York Giants	10/15/33	New York
PHOENIX CARDINALS (Chicago Cardinals)	Chicago Tigers	10/10/20	Chicago
PITTSBURGH STEELERS	New York Giants	9/20/33	Pittsburgh
SAN DIEGO CHARGERS (Los Angeles Chargers)	Dallas Texans	9/10/60	Los Angeles
SAN FRANCISCO 49ERS	New York Yankees	9/8/46	San Francisco
SEATTLE SEAHAWKS	St. Louis Cardinals	9/12/76	Seattle
TAMPA BAY BUCCANEERS	Houston Oilers	9/12/76	Houston
WASHINGTON REDSKINS (Boston Braves)	Brooklyn Dodgers	10/2/32	Boston

Super Bowl Results

	Super Bowl Winner	Loser	Score	Attendance
I	Green Bay Packers	Kansas City Chiefs	35–10	61,946
II	Green Bay Packers	Oakland Raiders	33–14	75,546
III	New York Jets	Baltimore Colts	16–7	75,389
IV	Kansas City Chiefs	Minnesota Vikings	23–7	80,562
V	Baltimore Colts	Miami Dolphins	16–13	79,204
VI	Dallas Cowboys	Miami Dolphins	24–3	81,023
VII	Miami Dolphins	Washington Redskins	14–7	90,182
VIII	Miami Dolphins	Minnesota Vikings	24–7	71,882
IX	Pittsburgh Steelers	Minnesota Vikings	16–6	80,997
X	Pittsburgh Steelers	Dallas Cowboys	21–17	80,187
XI	Oakland Raiders	Minnesota Vikings	32–14	103,438
XII	Dallas Cowboys	Denver Broncos	27–10	75,583
XIII	Pittsburgh Steelers	Dallas Cowboys	35–31	79,484
XIV	Pittsburgh Steelers	Los Angeles Rams	31–19	103,985
XV	Oakland Raiders	Philadelphia Eagles	27–10	76,135
XVI	San Francisco 49ers	Cincinnati Bengals	26–21	81,270
XVII	Washington Redskins	Miami Dolphins	27–17	103,667
XVIII	Los Angeles Raiders	Washington Redskins	38–9	72,920
XIX	San Francisco 49ers	Miami Dolphins	38–16	84,059
XX	Chicago Bears	New England Patriots	46–10	73,818
XXI	New York Giants	Denver Broncos	39–20	101,063
XXII	Washington Redskins	Denver Broncos	42–10	73,302
XXIII	San Francisco 49ers	Cincinnati Bengals	20–16	75,129
XXIV	San Francisco 49ers	Denver Broncos	55–10	72,919

Super Bowl MVP

Super Bowl I	Bart Starr, QB, Green Bay Packers
Super Bowl II	Bart Starr, QB, Green Bay Packers
Super Bowl III	Joe Namath, QB, New York Jets
Super Bowl IV	Len Dawson, QB, Kansas City Chiefs
Super Bowl V	Chuck Howley, LB, Dallas Cowboys
Super Bowl VI	Roger Staubach, QB, Dallas Cowboys
Super Bowl VII	Jake Scott, S, Miami
Super Bowl VIII	Larry Csonka, RB, Miami Dolphins
Super Bowl IX	Franco Harris, RB, Pittsburgh Steelers
Super Bowl X	Lynn Swann, WR, Pittsburgh Steelers
Super Bowl XI	Fred Biletnikoff, WR, Oakland Raiders
Super Bowl XII	Harvey Martin, DE, Randy White, DT, Dallas Cowboys
Super Bowl XIII	Terry Bradshaw, QB, Pittsburgh Steelers
Super Bowl XIV	Terry Bradshaw, QB, Pittsburgh Steelers
Super Bowl XV	Jim Plunkett, QB, Oakland Raiders
Super Bowl XVI	Joe Montana, QB, San Francisco 49ers
Super Bowl XVII	John Riggins, RB, Washington Redskins
Super Bowl XVIII	Marcus Allen, RB, Oakland Raiders
Super Bowl XIX	Joe Montana, QB, San Francisco 49ers
Super Bowl XX	Richard Dent, DE, Chicago Bears
Super Bowl XXI	Phil Simms, QB, New York Giants
Super Bowl XXII	Doug Williams, QB, Washington Redskins
Super Bowl XXIII	Jerry Rice, WR, San Francisco 49ers
Super Bowl XXIV	Joe Montana, QB, San Francisco 49ers

Pro Football's Mighty Mites

Name	Height	Team(s)
Jack Shapiro	5'½"	Staten Island Stapletons 1929
Reggie Smith	5'4"	Atlanta Falcons 1980–81
Buddy Young	5'5"	NY Yankees (AAFC) 1947–49; NY Yanks (NFL) 1950–51; Dallas Texans 1952; Baltimore Colts 1953–55
Howard Stevens	5'5"	New Orleans Saints 1973–74; Baltimore Colts 1975–77
Mack Herron	5'5"	New England Patriots 1973–75; Atlanta Falcons 1975
Mike Clemens	5'5"	Kansas City Chiefs 1987
Henry Homan	5'5½"	Frankford Yellow Jackets 1925–30
Charley Tolar	5'6"	Houston Oilers 1960–66
Jack Larscheid	5'6"	Oakland Raiders 1960–61
Nolan Smith	5'6"	Kansas City Chiefs 1967–69; San Francisco 49ers 1969
Stanley Rosen	5'6"	Buffalo Bisons 1929
Lionel James	5'6"	San Diego Chargers 1984–89
Jim Breech	5'6"	Oakland Raiders 1978–79; Cincinnati Bengals 1980–88
Ed Scharer	5'6½"	Detroit Panthers 1926; Pottsville Maroons 1927; Detroit Wolverines 1928

The Other Leagues

1926 American Football League

Philadelphia Quakers
New York Yankees
Cleveland Panthers
Los Angeles Wildcats
Chicago Bulls
Boston Bulldogs
Rock Island Independents
Brooklyn Horsemen
Newark Bears

1936–37
American Football League

1936
Boston Shamrocks
Cleveland Rams
New York Yankees
Pittsburgh Americans
Rochester Tigers
Brooklyn Tigers

1937
Los Angeles Bulldogs
Rochester Tigers
New York Yankees
Cincinnati Bengals
Boston Shamrocks
Pittsburgh Americans

1940–41
American Football League

1940
Columbus Bullies
Milwaukee Chiefs
Boston Bears
New York Yankees
Buffalo Indians
Cincinnati Bengals

1941
Columbus Bullies
New York Americans
Milwaukee Chiefs
Buffalo Indians
Cincinnati Bengals

1946–49
All-America Football Conference

1946
Eastern Division
New York Yankees
Brooklyn Dodgers
Buffalo Bisons
Miami Seahawks

Western Division
Cleveland Browns
San Francisco 49ers
Los Angeles Dons
Chicago Rockets

1947
Eastern Division
New York Yankees
Buffalo Bills
Brooklyn Dodgers
Baltimore Colts

Western Division
Cleveland Browns
San Francisco 49ers
Los Angeles Dons
Chicago Rockets

1948
Eastern Division
Buffalo Bills
Baltimore Colts
New York Yankees
Brooklyn Dodgers

Western Division
Cleveland Browns
San Francisco 49ers
Los Angeles Dons
Chicago Rockets

1949
Cleveland Browns
San Francisco 49ers
Brooklyn-New York Yankees
Buffalo Bills
Chicago Hornets
Los Angeles Dons
Baltimore Colts

1974–75 World Football League

1974
Eastern Division
Florida Blazers
New York Stars/Charlotte
 Hornets
Philadelphia Bell
Jacksonville Sharks

Central Division
Memphis Southmen
Birmingham Americans
Chicago Fire
Detroit Wheels

Western Division
Southern California Sun
Hawaiians
Portland Storm
Houston Texans/Shreveport
 Steamer

1975
Eastern Division
Birmingham Vulcans
Memphis Southmen
Charlotte Hornets
Jacksonville Express
Philadelphia Bell

Western Division
Southern California Sun
San Antonio Wings
Shreveport Steamer
Hawaiians
Portland Thunder
Chicago Winds

1983–85
United States Football League

1983
Pacific Division
Oakland Invaders
Los Angeles Express
Denver Gold
Arizona Wranglers

Central Division
Michigan Panthers
Chicago Blitz
Tampa Bay Bandits
Birmingham Stallions

Atlantic Division
Philadelphia Stars
Boston Breakers
New Jersey Generals
Washington Federals

1984
Eastern Conference
Atlantic Division
Philadelphia Stars
New Jersey General
Pittsburgh Maulers
Washington Federals

Southern Division
Birmingham Stallions
Tampa Bay Bandits
New Orleans Breakers
Memphis Showboats
Jacksonville Bulls

Western Conference
Central Division
Houston Gamblers
Michigan Panthers
San Antonio Gunslingers
Oklahoma Outlaws
Chicago Blitz

Pacific Division
Los Angeles Express
Arizona Wranglers
Denver Gold
Oakland Invaders

1985
Eastern Conference
Birmingham Stallions
New Jersey Generals
Memphis Showboats
Baltimore Stars
Tampa Bay Bandits
Jacksonville Bulls
Orlando Renegades

Western Conference
Oakland Invaders
Denver Gold
Houston Gamblers
Arizona Outlaws
Portland Breakers
San Antonio Gunslingers
Los Angeles Express